DIRTY
KOREAN

DIRTY
KOREAN

EVERYDAY SLANG FROM
"WHAT'S UP?" TO "F*%# OFF!"

•••••Haewon Geebi Baek

Illustrated by Lindsay Mack

 Ulysses Press

Published by:
Ulysses Press
P.O. Box 3440
Berkeley, CA 94703
www.ulyssespress.com

ISBN: 978-1-56975-779-6
Library of Congress Control Number: 2009940343

Printed in Canada by Webcom

10 9 8 7 6 5 4 3

Acquisitions editor: Kelly Reed
Managing editor: Claire Chun
Editors: Nick Denton-Brown, J. Han
Production: Abigail Reser
Proofreader: Lauren Harrison
Interior design: what!design @ whatweb.com
Cover design: Double R Design
Front cover photo: woman © bigstockphoto.com/WizData
Back cover illustration: Lindsay Mack

Distributed by Publishers Group West

This book is dedicated, of course, to my one and only sis, 혜진언니

TABLE OF CONTENTS

·····Acknowledgments

I would like to thank acquisitions editor Kelly Reed for giving me the opportunity to write this book. I could not have finished this project without her words of encouragement during my bouts of writer's block and procrastination. I also want to thank two exchange students from Korea, Gyungbae Jeon and Dong-guen Kim Oppas, who came to my rescue and supplied some cool new slang terms that I've gladly added to the book. I must thank my parents (I am Korean, albeit a hyphenated "American," who still values family and the traditional wisdom they've instilled in me), especially my dad, for his sense of humor that I've enjoyed and embraced over the years. Thanks to Matt Kent, Gene Desmidt, Miyo Nakamura, Borami Lee, Krissy McClelland, Jeffrey Ezell, Drew Dibble, Analisa Lono and Lauren Adelman, my best friends, for believing in me.

Most importantly, I'll be super grateful for the rest of my life to Jinny Baek, my awesome sister. The knowledge she gathered during the two years she spent teaching English in Korea proved to be invaluable. She corrected and refined my work, which would have been dull and humorless if she hadn't spent the time reviewing the manuscript and rewrites. (You can tell that she's standing right next to me dictating the words as I type.)

Last, I thank you, the readers, who are so curious about the Korean language that you've bought this little primer. Yes, you have the right to learn how to say, "Let's have sex!" or "Suck my dick!" in Korean!

USING THIS BOOK

Whether you're an exchange-student headed to Korea to study and broaden your worldview, or a frat bro looking to drink your ass off and feed your raging case of Yellow Fever, you're gonna need to know more than just how to say "hi" and "thank you." You need to be able to order a drink, pick up a date and tell a douchebag to go "suck on your mama's titties" more (*ssibalnom, gaseo eomma jeot-ina deo bbaldawa*; 씨발놈, 가서 엄마 젓이나 더 빨다와)!

This book is designed to teach you all those sorts of words, the ones that your professors were too scared to teach you, those phrases too raunchy to appear in any textbook and all those expressions you would never, ever say in front of your mother—in short, all the sayings that you actually give a shit about. Because let's be honest, when was the last time you were hanging out with friends and felt the need to say "I live in the red house. I enjoy tennis. Where is the library?" Nobody talks this way, least of all Koreans, who—once they warm up to you—can be some of the most foulmouthed motherfuckers you'll ever meet. So let's get real for a change.

Dirty Korean is the product of a lifetime of vulgar language picked up from lots of bad company and many a poor life choice—none of which I regret today, however, because it all led to this little gem of a book that I now pass on to you, dear reader. Use it wisely and at your own peril.

It's been arranged thematically, and each English phrase is followed by its Korean pronunciation and written characters. I've also included important and interesting tidbits on Korean culture to give you a better understanding of the phrases, places and social customs you'll encounter during your travels. That's because I'd hate to have you mistake a sarcastic pickup line for a verbal slap-in-the-face and lose your chance at baggin' some hottie. So now, go forth—take your *Dirty Korean* and get dirty with it!

·····Quick and Dirty Korean Pronunciation

Korean is super easy to read and write once you master the 24 characters that, when put together, make the sounds of the Korean language. If you're a quick learner, you'll probably master them in about an hour. The letters are all geometric shapes that were created by King Sejong in the 1400s.

TONES

To most foreigners, Korean just sounds angry or whiny. Koreans tend to speak with a stiff intonation, as opposed to the more fluid sounds of English speakers. One way to practice your Korean accent is to drag your tongue at the end of your syllables to make the sounds a little whinier (the tilde after the *hangeul* means you should drag out the syllable).

> Annyeong~
> 안녕~

CONSONANTS

The Korean alphabet has 14 consonants that are similar to those in English. However, there are double consonants that are pronounced differently. Whenever you see doubled letters, make sure to speak with a strong emphasis that almost make you sound angry.

ㄱ = **g**, **k**, like in "gorgeous" / ㄲ = kk

ㄴ = **n**, like in "norm"

ㄷ = **d**, **t**, like in "drum" / ㄸ = dd, tt

ㄹ = **r**, **l**, like in "rude"

ㅁ = **m**, like in "morning"

ㅂ = **b**, **p**, like in "breasts" / ㅃ = **bb** like in "pepper"

ㅅ = **s**, like in "sex"/ㅆ = ss

ㅇ = **ng**, like in "meeting" (but silent if at the beginning of the word)

ㅈ = **j**, like in "joy"/ㅉ = jj

ㅊ = **ch**, like in "chihuahua"

ㅋ = **k**, like in "key"

ㅌ = **t**, like in "toy"

ㅍ = **p**, like in "punch"

ㅎ = **h**, like in "horny"

VOWELS

The Korean dialect has 10 vowels. It can be difficult to pronounce them at first because of the subtle similarity of their sounds. But once you get to hang of it, it's pretty easy.

HOW TO READ KOREAN)))

Korean can be written in either the standard Western style (left to right in horizontal rows) or in vertical columns reading from top to bottom and right to left, although the latter is rarely used nowadays.

When actually reading the characters, remember that letters (consonants and vowels) never stand alone—consonants are always combined with a vowel (or a vowel and another consonant) to form syllable blocks. These blocks always start with a consonant followed by a vowel to the right of or beneath it. Note: When the consonant ㅇ is placed at the beginning of a block, it's silent.

You pronounce the sound of each letter in a syllable block from left to right first, then read any letters that are at the bottom half of the block. The bottom letters are called *batchim* (받침), supporting consonants used at the end of a syllable block to form the sound. For example, 한글 (*hangeul*). It reads:

ㅎ (h)

ㅏ (a)

ㄴ (n)

ㄱ (g)

— (eu)

ㄹ (l)

Then try and 쉽다 (*swipda*) = ㅅ (s), ㅟ (wi), ㅂ (p), ㄷ (d), ㅏ (a). You just said 한글쉽다, which means "Korean is easy!" The learning's gonna be so fast that you'll be ordering *soju* and negotiating with a prostitute in no time!

ㅏ = **a**, like in "father"

ㅑ = **ya**, like in "yahoo"

ㅓ = **eo**, like in "fuck"

ㅕ = **yeo**, like in "y'all"

ㅗ = **oh**, like in "old"

ㅛ = **yo**, like in "yo mama"

ㅜ = **u**, like in "moon"

ㅠ = **yu**, like in "you"

─ = **eu**, there is no sound like this in English. Just put your teeth together and pull your lips while you try to make this vowel sound.

ㅣ = **i**, like in "lily" or "silly"

Also, Korean vowels combine to make different sounds such as,

ㅐ (ㅏ + ㅣ) = **ae**, like in "bayer"

ㅒ (ㅑ + ㅣ) = **yae**, like in "yeah"

ㅔ (ㅓ + ㅣ) = **e**, like in "never"

ㅖ (ㅕ + ㅣ) = **ye**, like in "Yale"

ㅘ (ㅗ + ㅏ) = **wa**, like in "wash"

ㅙ (ㅗ + ㅐ) = **wae**, like in "whey"

ㅚ (ㅗ + ㅣ) = **oe**, also like in "whey"

ㅝ (ㅜ + ㅓ) = **wo**, like in "woman"

ㅞ (ㅜ + ㅔ) = **we**, like in "wedding"

ㅟ (ㅜ + ㅣ) = **wi**, like in "wing"

ㅢ (─ + ㅣ) = **ui**, like in "ooh-ee"

CHAPTER 1

HOWDY KOREAN
HANGUK INSAMAL
한국 인사말

•••••Hello
Annyeonghaseyo
안녕하세요

Unlike some languages, it's cool to use Korean slang with complete strangers. But only if you're older than they are. If you're not, or it's questionable, you best stick to formalities and old-fashioned "hellos." Korea is just age-deferential like that. If you're with friends though, all bets are off—feel free to get slangy as you wanna be.

Hi (to same age or younger)
Annyeong
안녕

Yo!
Ya!
야!

Hey!
Imma!
인마!

Good to see ya.
Banga banga.
방가 방가.

On the phone:

Hello?
Yeoboseyo?
여보세요?

Who dis?
Nuguseyo?
누구세요?

•••••What's up?
Wannya? / Wasseo?
왔냐? / 왔어?

Like in any language, you always gotta find out how your peeps been doin' when you haven't seen 'em in a while. Don't be too surprised, though, when Koreans talk bluntly about how fat your ass has gotten since they last saw you. Changes to your physical appearance are considered fair game for discussion. Don't be offended. It just is what it is, fatty.

How ya been?
Jal jinaeni?
잘 지내니?

Yeah, I'm good!
Eung, jal jinae!
응, 잘 지내!

Good!
Joa!
좋아!

So-so.
Geunyang geurae.
그냥 그래.

Sucky.
Guryeo.
구려.

Whatcha been up to?
Mohago sarannya?
뭐하고 살았냐?

Long time no see!
Oretmaniyeyo!
오랫만이예요!

It's been a while.
Olman!
올만!

You're still alive?
Saraisseonnya?
살아있었냐?

You need to lose some weight!
Sal jom bbaeyagetda!
살 좀 빼야겠다!

Your face has gotten chubbier!
Eolguli tongtonghae!
얼굴이 통통해!

Your mom has gotten chubbier!
Neone eomma saljom jjisyeosseo!
너네 엄마 살좀 찌셨어!

·····Goodbye
Jal jinae~
잘 지내~

You know how in Hawaiian aloha means both "hi" and "bye"? Well, Korean is the same way. You just have to drag out the end of the word "hello" to make the difference.

Goodbye (general use)
Annyeong~
안녕~

Goodbye (to a person staying)
Jal isseo~
잘 있어~

Goodbye (to a person leaving)
Jal ga~
잘 가~

Goodbye (when both parties are parting)
Jal jinae~
잘 지내~
Literally, "be well."

Bye bye
Bai bai
바이 바이

See ya!
Tto boja!
또 보자!

Later!
Najungebwa!
나중에봐!

I'm out.
Na ganda.
나 간다.

Be careful!
Josimhae!
조심해!

·····G'morning!
Joeun achim!
좋은 아침!

The formal ways of saying "good morning" and "good evening" are so long-winded that you might pass out trying to say them in one breath. Better not to risk it. Stick with the more casual ways of greeting friends and family.

Good morning (formal)
Annyeonghi jumusyeoseoyo
안녕히 주무셨어요

G'morning!
Joeun achim!
좋은 아침!

Sleep well?
Jal jasseo?
잘잤어?

It's a beautiful evening!
Joeun bam!
좋은 밤!

Good evening (formal)
Annyeonghi jumuseyo
안녕히 주무세요

Evenin'
Jaja~
잘자~

Sweet dreams!
Joeun kkumkkwo!
좋은 꿈꿔!

Dream about me!
Nae kkumkkwo!
내 꿈꿔!

·····I am sorry
Mianhapnida
미안합니다

Let's be honest: Apologizing blows. And you usually don't even mean it. But it's one of those things that you have to know how to do, even if it's bullshit. But if you have to do it, you might as well have some fun with it.

Sorry! (informal)
Mian!
미안!

Forgive me!
Yongseohaejwo!
용서해줘!

Oops!
At!
앗!

My bad!
Silsu!
실수!

No worries.
Geokjeonghajima~.
걱정하지마~.

It's all good.
Da gwaenchana.
다 괜찮아.

No problem.
Munjae eopsseo.
문제없어.

Forget about it.
Ljeobeoryeo.
잊어버려.

Well excuuuuse me for living!
Jugeuljoereuljyeotda!
죽을 죄를 졌다!
Literally, "I have committed a killing sin!" and is said sarcastically,
as in "I'm soooo sorry for what I've done to deserve to DIE!"

•••••Please
Budi / Jebal
부디 / 제발

Koreans don't really use the word "please" unless it's in an
extremely formal setting or out of sheer desperation ("Please
don't sodomize me with that rusty ice pick, Sir"). Because
"please" isn't used much in their language, Koreans are often
thought to be rude or demanding when they're in the States.
But they're not; it's just their language.

Can you please scratch my back?
*Nae deung **jom** geulgeojullae?*
내 등 **좀** 긁어줄래?
When Koreans ask for something politely, they say the word little
(*jom*; 좀), instead of please.

Can you please do me a favor?
Budi butak jom deureojullae?
부디 부탁 좀 들어줄래?

Please, accept my heart!
Jebal je mameul badajuseyo!
제발 제 맘을 받아주세요!

·····Making friends
Chingu mandeulgi
친구 만들기

If you want to make friends in Korea, you don't go up to strangers and just start talking to them. That's creepy. Instead, you meet people through internet clubs such as meetup.com or through Facebook events. Also, you can make friends at different clubs in Hongdae or Itaewon while you get drunk and dance with strangers. If you're looking to hook up, clubs are definitely the way to go. Korean girls will throw themselves at

EXCUSE ME)))
SILLYEHAPNIDA / JAMSIMANYO
식례합니다 / 잔시만요

"Excuse me" can be used as an apology or for asking a favor. But don't worry about saying "excuse me" every time you bump into someone in Korea. It's a small country with a high density of people. Shit happens. Just keep walking and pretend like it never happened. Also, don't get offended if some ol' ladies bump into you or cut you off in a subway line. They're trained to be like that all through their existence. These *ajummas*, old ladies, are all like that. Be the better person and smile! Or you can cuss them out and give them a finger. Your choice.

> Excuse me
> *Sillyehapnida / Jamsimanyo*
> 식례합니다 / 잔시만요
> Literally, "one minute," but you can use this one to get through the crazy crowds in Korea.

> Cuse' me
> *Sillye~*
> 식례~

> Move out of my way!
> *Bikyeo!*
> 비켜!

> Be careful!
> *Josim!*
> 조심!

INTRODUCING YOURSELF)))
JAGI SOGAE
자기 소개

My name is James.
Nae ireumeun James ipnida.
제 이름은 제임스 입니다.

I am from America.
Jeoneun eseo wasseupnida.
저는 미국에서 왔습니다.

I have yellow fever.
Jeoneun donyanginman joahapnida.
저는 동양인만 좋아합니다.

I am 18 years old and full of testosterone.
Jeoneun yeollyeodeolssaligo himi neomchipnida.
저는 역여덟살이고 힘이 넘칩니다.

I like hairy girls.
Jeoneun teol maneun yeojaga josseupnida.
저는 턱 많은 여자가 좋습니다.

you if you are a foreigner. They want to learn English and see the big sausages as a bonus. Show them what you've got! It's easier to get laid if you have friends to back you up. So take your fugly wingmen out with you to take the fugly girls out of the equation.

Meeting
Miting
미팅

These are the occasions where a bunch of girls and boys meet for a date, usually for high school and college students.

Hey, is there a meeting you can set up?
Ya, mitingjari eopsseo?
야, 미팅자리 없어?

Do you have someone you picked?
Jjigeun ae isseo?
찍은 애 있어?

Blind date
Sogaeting
소개팅

Can you set me up on a **blind date** with one of your hottie friends?
*Jal saeng-gin chingurang na **sogaeting** sikyeojo?*
잘 생긴 친구랑 나 **소개팅** 시켜줘?

Arranged blind date
Seon
선

A long time ago, all Koreans had arranged marriages. Although most people marry out of love nowadays, there still are a few Koreans who are forced by their parents to go through arranged blind dates to meet the "right kind of the other half."

Nice to meet you.
Mannaseo ban-gapseupnida.
만나서 반갑습니다.

What's your name?
Ireumi mwoyeyo?
이름이 뭐예요?

Have we met before?
Uri mannanjeok itnayo?
우리 만난적 있나요?

Do you have a light?
Laita isseuseyo?
라이터 있으세요?

Do you have the time?
Jigeum myeossiyeyo?
지금 몇시예요?

How old are you?
Naiga eotteoke dwae?
나이가 어떻게 돼?

Really? You don't look that old!
Jeongmal? Geureoke an boyeo~!
정말? 그렇게 안 보여~!

Me, too! I'm the same age!
Nado dong-gap!
나도 동갑!

Let's not talk so formally.
Uri mal noeulkkayo? / Uri yaja tteullkka?
우리 말 놓을까요? / 우리 야자 뜰까?

Do you come here often?
Yeogi jajuwa?
여기 자주와?

Do you want to get a drink?
Uri sul hanjan halkka?
우리 술 한잔 할까?

Where are you from?
Eodiseo wasseo?
어디서 왔어?

Where do you live?
Eodi sara?
어디 살아?

Let's be friends.
Uri chingu halkka?
우리 친구 할까?

What's your phone number?
Jeonhwabeonhoga mwoya?
전화번호가 뭐야?

What is your Cyworld address?
Cy jusoga eottoke dwae?
싸이 주소가 어떻게 돼?
Cyworld is a social-networking site, like the Facebook of Korea.

Let's go have sex?
Uri enjoy halkka?
우리 인조이 할까?
Literally, "let's enjoy tonight."

·····Pictures
Sajin
사진

Since the digital camera revolution, Koreans have become obsessed with taking pictures. You'll have to be patient when they take pics of their meals before they eat at restaurants, which has become something of a tradition. You can't touch the food before the girls take pictures of it! They'll chop your hands off, so be careful. And if you want to take a photo of some of your Korean friends, know that Koreans have a huge complex about their head/face size. It's common to see people fight over who gets to stand in the background of a portrait to make their head look smaller than everybody else's. That's also why you might see people covering their cheeks with a hand or bangs. And when you pose, don't forget to make the V-for-Victory sign with your hand before the shutter snaps!

Digital camera
Dika
디카

> **Fuck digital cameras! Mechanical cameras are the best!**
> *Dijitaleun gaebbul! Sudongi joa!*
> 디지털은 개뿔! 수동이 좋아!

Self-taking picture skill
Selka
셀카

Yes, Koreans have a word for this. Even with their short arms they can actually get about four to five people in the picture, including themselves. The best angle for the self-taking pictures according to Koreans is 45 degrees up from your face.

Cell phone camera
Phoneka
폰카

Let's take a picture!
Sajin jjikja!
사진 찍자!

Can you take a picture of me?
Sajin jjigeo juseyo.
사진 찍어 주세요.

"One, two, three"
Hana, dul, set
하나 둘 셋

Cheese
Kimchi~
김치~

Saying *kimchi* is like saying "cheese" when taking a picture in Korea. You can say it to make the perfect smiling face in a picture. This is a must-do, along with the V-for-Victory (or peace sign), when you take pictures.

CHAPTER 2

FRIENDLY KOREAN
HANGUK CHINGUKKIRI HANEUNMAL
한국 친구끼리 하는말

If your only exposure to Koreans is the Hollywood stereotype of a pissed-off liquor store owner with a gun, you may think all Koreans have a bug up their ass. You'd be wrong—Koreans are warm and affectionate people…once you get to know them. But first you'll have to break through the sometimes forceful and angry sounds of the language. If you can do that, you'll find yourself well on your way to some lasting friendships.

•••••Friends
Chingudeul
친구들

Most Koreans have a ton of different friends and acquaintances, and they have a pupu platter of words they use to describe those different relationships. It's no different in the States, really. After all, here you've got your BF or GF, your BFF, your booty call, your homies, your Facebook friends, and, of course, your WoW avatar friends, who aren't actually real people, let alone real friends.

Friend
Chingu
친구

> **Are you my real friend?**
> *Neo jinjja nae **chingu** maja?*
> 너 진짜 내 **친구** 맞아?

Total stranger
Moreuneun saram / Cheoeum bon saram
모르는 사람 / 처음 본 사람

> **That total stranger smiled all creepy at me!**
> ***Cheom bo neun sarami** nabogo jingeurupge useosseo!*
> **첨 보는 사람**이 나보고 징그럽게 웃었어!

Acquaintance
Aneun saram
아는 사람

> **She's just an acquaintance from school.**
> *Hakgyoeseo geunyang **aneun saramiya**.*
> 학교에서 그냥 **아는 사람**이야.

Classmate
Ban chingu
반 친구

> **My stoner classmate was suspended for smoking weed in math class.**
> *Nae gateun**ban chingu**ga suhaksiganae daemachopida jeonghak danghaesseo.*
> 내 같은**반 친구**가 수학시간에 대마초피다 정학당했어.

Coworker
Hoesa dongryo
회사동묘

My coworker is slacking and giving me all his work.
Nae hoesa dongiga jakku ireul nahante tteo neomgyeo.
내 **회사 동기**가 자꾸 일을 나한테 떠 넘겨.

Homey
Bural chingu
불알 친구

Literally, "testicle friends," i.e., you've been friends since you were babies when it was all good to see each other's nutsacks. To be used among men only.

He's my homey.
Nae bural chinguya.
내 **불알친구**야.

Next-door neighbor
Yeopjip chingu / iut
옆집 친구 / 이웃

My next-door neighbor is like family.
Nae yupjip sarameun nae iut sachoniji.
내 옆집사람은 내 **이웃사촌**이지.

Literally, "neighbor cousin."

Friends from same town
Dongnae chingu
동내 친구

Study buddy
Gateun gwa chingu
같은 과 친구

This is used for university students referring to friends from the same major.

School friend
Hakgyo chingu
학교 친구

Housemate
Dongeoin
동거인

My housemate farts all day long.
*Nae **dongeoin** bangu mennal kkyeo.*
내 **동거인** 방구 맨날껴.

Roomie
Bangjjak
방짝

Hey roomie, stop eating my kimchi and buy your own!
*Ya, **bangjjak**, nae kimchi meokjimalgo neokkeo sameogeo!*
야 **방짝**, 내 김치 먹지말고 너꺼 사먹어!

BFF (mainly used by girls in grade school)
Danjjak
단짝

Best friend
Jeil chinhan chingu
제일 친한 친구

Partner (someone who sits next to you in grade school)
Jjakgung
짝궁

In Korean elementary schools, students have to sit two abreast in assigned seats. You're stuck with your partner for a whole semester unless the teacher decides to make a seating change. This leads to territorial behavior for your rightful half of the desk, usually demarcated by an invisible line you draw smack dab in the middle. So if your eraser crosses into your partner's domain, the eraser gets cut in half. Be careful where you put your finger.

Business work partner
Dongeopja
동업자

Soulmate
Cheongsaengyeonbun
천생연분

Crush
Jjaksarang
짝사랑

> **I have a crush.**
> *Na **jjaksarang** hagoisseo.*
> 나 **짝사랑** 하고있어.

Lovers
Aein
애인

> **Aren't we lovers now?**
> *Uri ije **aein** aniya?*
> 우리 이제 **애인** 아니야?

Boyfriend
Namjachingu
남자친구

> **Do you have a boyfriend?**
> ***Namjachingu** isseo?*
> **남자친구** 있어?

BF
Namchin
남친

Girlfriend
Yeojachingu
여자친구

GF
Yeohchin
여친

Traitor
Baesinja
배신자

> **Hey, you traitor!**
> *Ya, i **baesinja**ya!*
> 야 이 **배신자**야!

Dude
Imma / Jjasik
인마 / 자식

> **Dude, where's my car?**
> ***Imma**, nae cha eodinnya?*
> **인마**, 내 차 어딧냐?

·····Family
Gajok
가족

Family is extremely important to Korean culture. It's just recently that the divorce rate has gone up, resulting in all different types of family dynamics. However, you can't just ignore the old saying, "Blood is thicker than water." Koreans put their family matters before any other business. That's why in some Korean soap operas, a girl might have a baby with a guy she's just met to fulfill a dying grandma's wish ("Tada! Here's your grandson, even though I hate the husband you arranged for me!"). Korean society is heavy-duty with showing respect for elders. At school, being just one year older really creates a huge inequality among students of different ages — it gives the older students the right to lord over the younger ones. They may order the "youngsters" around and even bully the poor little souls into doing anything they want. Maybe that's why Korean people can bluntly ask you "How old are you?" the first minute you meet them.

Mother
Eomeoni
어머니

Mom
Eomma
엄마

> **I swear on my mom being a prostitute if it's not true.**
> *I yaksok an jikimyeon eommchang!*
> 이 약속 안 지키면 **엄창**!
> Koreans don't have "yo mama" jokes. But when they swear on something important, they swear it on their mother being a prostitute.

Father
Abeoji
아버지

Dad
Abba
아빠

Grandmother
Halmeoni
할머니

When Grandma comes up in conversation, Koreans distinguish which side of the family (mom's or dad's) their grandparent represents. Dad's mom is called *chinhalmeoni* (친할머니), while mom's mom is referred to as *woehalmeoni* (외할머니).

Grandma
Halmae
할매

This is more affectionate and is used in rural areas.

SiBLiNG RiVALRY)))

It's considered rude to call your older siblings by their first name. Instead you have to use their honorific titles "Brother" or "Sister." But it's all good for older siblings to call their younger siblings by their first names. Even if a twin sister is just two minutes younger, she still has to address her elder wombmate as "Sister." This curious bit of culture led to the following exchange in *Mary Kate and Ashley Go to Seoul*:

"Mary Kate?"
Mary Kate?
"메리 케이트?"

"Yes, Sister?"
Wae eonni?
"왜, 언니?"

"Get me my bulimia bucket!"
Na tohage yangdongijom gajigo wa!
"나 토하게 양동이좀 가지고 와!"

[Mary Kate is extremely unhappy about this.]
[Mary Katega ashleyreul bogo hwareul naenda.]
(메리 케이트가 에쉬리를 보고 화를 낸다.)

Brother (what a girl calls her older brother)
Obba
오빠

Brother (what a boy calls his older brother)
Hyeong
형

Sister (what a girl calls her older sister)
Eonni
언니

Sister (what a boy calls his older sister)
Nuna
누나

Younger sibling
Dongsaeng
동생

Younger brother / Younger sister
Namdongsaeng / Yeodongsaeng
남동생 / 여동생

Grandfather
Harabeoji
할아버지

As mentioned above, when discussing Grandpa's noisy farts with friends, be sure to clarify if you're talking about your pop's pop (*chinharabeoji*; 친할아버지) or your mama's papa (*woeharabeoji*; 외할아버지).

Grandpa
Halbae
할배

Stepmother / Stepfather
Sae-eomma / Saeabba
새엄마 / 새아빠

•••••Titles
Hocching
호칭

Like with your siblings, it's considered disrespectful to call someone older than you by their first name. So titles like Mr., Mrs. or Miss are typically used when you're not sure of the other person's age or assume they're older than you. This can get you into trouble, though, if you end up addressing a girl with a title when she's actually younger than you. In effect, you've basically called her an old-looking hag and have ruined any chance you had of ever hooking up with her. Congratulations.

The title game is dangerous ground; tread lightly. These ruinous pitfalls can be avoided by calling every woman you may want to sleep with "sweet thang" (*eepeuni*; 이쁜이). Nothing can possibly go wrong by doing this!

Mr.
Ajeossi
아저씨

Mr. (not married)
Chongak
종각
Used by older women.

Mrs.
Ajumma
아줌마
This term doesn't always refer to married women; it can also be used pejoratively for someone who just looks like a middle-aged housewife.

Miss
Agassi
아가씨
This is a woman who looks like she is between the age of a university student and a 30-something.

·····Everyday people
Maeilboneun saramdeul
매일보는 사람들

Let's face it, you spend most of your life either in school or working. Yeah, maybe you get a couple of brief retirement years in the sun afterward, but by that point you're already on your way out and drinking Ensure through a straw for dinner while your caretaker wipes the dribble off your chin. So here are a few of the people you'll meet every day on your journey through life as a student or worker in Korea.

CEO / Boss
Sajangnim
사장님

> My **boss** is a real prick.
> *Uri **sajangnim**eun jinjja jaesuya.*
> 우리 **사장님**은 진짜 재수야.

Secretary
Biseo
비서

The secretary is sleeping her way to the top.
Sajangi jeo biseorang baramnaseo seungjinhaennabwa.
사장이 저 **비서**랑 바람나서 승진했나봐.

Blue collar
Nodongja
노동자

That CEO looks hella blue collar!
Jeo sajangeun dondo maneunde nodongja gachi eolguri sikkeomae!
저 사장은 돈도 많은데 **노동자** 같이 얼굴이 시꺼매!

Owner
Juin
주인

Store owners are such tight asses.
Gagye juindeureun jeongmal ssagajiya.
가게 **주인들**은 정말 싸가지야.

Customer
Sonnim
손님

The customer is always right.
Sonnimeun wangiya.
손님은 왕이야.

Government workers
Gongmuwon
공무원

Government workers can't do anything right.
Gongmuwon saekkideul haljulaneunge hanado eopsseo.
공무원 새끼들 할줄아는게 하나도 없어.

Military solider
Gunin
군인
It's every Korean man's duty to serve in the military for two years.

Korean soldiers think they're such hot shit.
Hanguk gunindeureun jideuri chwegoinjool ara.
한국 군인들은 지들이 쳐고인줄 알아.

Yankees (American soldiers)
Migun
미군
There are thousands of American military members stationed in Korea. They often stick out in a crowd with their high, tight haircuts and loud, drunken antics in bars. There has been tension between Koreans and American soldiers, but now the attitude is of general acceptance.

All the **Yankees** are drunken meatheads.
Migun sekkideureun da sulchwihan gogideongeoriya.
미군 새끼들은 다 술취한 고깃덩어리야.

·····Student life
Hakchangsijeol
학창시절

Teacher
Sunsaengnim
선생님
Koreans highly value educated people and it's their passion to get as much education as possible. Being a tutor is one of the most popular jobs in Korea, especially for university students. You're called "teacher" even if you're just tutoring.

I wanna bone my **teacher**.
Uri ssaem irang neomu hagosipeo.
우리 쌤이랑 너무 하고싶어.

Teach! (noun)
Ssaem!
쌤!
Don't use this term with uptight teachers.

Yo, Teach. Let's get our learn on.
Eoi, Ssaem, jom baewo bojago.
어이, **쌤**, 좀 배워보자고.

Tutor
Gwawoe sunsaeng
과외 선생

My tutor is useless shit head!
Nae gwawoe sunsaengeun sseulmoeopneun meongcheongiya!
내 **과외선생**은 쓸모없는 멍청이야!

Student
Haksaeng
학생

Senior (in school)
Sunbae
선배

One year of age makes a huge difference in Korea. If you are a grade above your fellow students, you get to use them like slaves!

The senior is using me like a slave.
Sunbaega na ddonggaehullyeon sikyeo.
선배가 나 똥개훈련 씨켜.

Freshman
Hubae
후배

As a student at the bottom of the age totem pole, you may suffer a bit from senior bullies. But don't worry, your time will come, too!

Freshmen don't know shit.
Hubaedeureun jinjja amugeotdo moreunda.
후배들은 진짜 아무것도 모른다.

High school kid
Goding
고딩

Is it wrong to be attracted to high schoolers?
Godinghante banhamyeon andwaena?
고딩한테 반하면 안돼나?

Middle school kid
Jungding
중딩

> Who's the creeper hanging around the **middle school kids**?
> *Jeo **jungding**yeopae dagaoneun byeontae nugunya?*
> 저 **중딩**옆에 다가오는 변태 누구냐?

Elementary school kid
Choding
초딩

> Little **elementary kids** are always so snotty.
> *Jwisekkimanhan **choding**deuri hangsang kkabureo.*
> 쥐새끼만한 **초딩**들이 항상 까불어.

·····Characters
Gaeseongjeogin hangukin
개성적인 한국인

Unlike America's cowboy, go-it-alone mentality, Korea is very much a group society. You can almost always put anyone into the group they belong in and label them accordingly. Koreans won't be insulted if you stereotype them based on who they hang out with. They feel more comfortable being defined by groups than as individuals. This can be confusing or insulting to politically correct American ears, but it's a real timesaver in Korea.

Bookworm
Gongbubeollae
공부벌래

Student
Haksaeng
학생

Airhead
Golbinnom / Nyeon
골빈놈 / 년

Wannabe ganster

Yangachi

양아치

These are immature teenager boys who spend their parents' money on their looks and act like tough, wannabe gansters.

Ditz

Nallari

날라리

This is a teenager more interested in appearances than studies.

Snob

Sokmul

속물

Bean paste girl (gold digger)

Doenjangnyeo

된장녀

This term comes from someone who can't distinguish shit from bean paste! A bean paste girl is typically superficial, shallow, materialistic and obsessed with brand-name goods. Some even use their parents' or sugar daddy/mama's money to buy stuff to make themselves look glamorous. Because they're so blinded by brand names, they're ill-equipped to make judgment calls on the actual quality of an item. Therefore, they would even purchase shit if they hear it's a brand-name bean paste.

The bean paste girl has yet another Gucci bag.

Jeo doenjangnyeo tto Gucci bag deurunne.

저 **된장녀** 또 구찌백 들었네.

Pepper paste boy

Gochujangnam

고추장남

This term applies to boys who have the same qualities as bean paste girls. The word *gochoo* (고추), a Korean red-hot pepper, is a homonym for penis *eumkyeong* (음경). Thus the gender-specific twist!

Businessperson
Hoesawon
회사원

> Both my parents are **businesspeople** who work for LG.
> *Uri bumonim dulda LG **hoesawoniya**.*
> 우리 부모님 둘다 엘지 **회사원**이야.

Biracial
Honhyeora
혼혈아

Foreigner
Woegukin
외국인

> Just learn to speak Korean, already, you dumb **foreigner**!
> *Ah, hangukkmallohae meongcheonghan **weogukin**a!*
> 아, 한국말로해, 멍청한 **외국인**아!

Bum
Geoji
거지

> Fuck, I am sick of giving money to **bums**.
> *Sibal, **geojideul**hante donjuneungeo jonna akkawo.*
> 시발, **거지들**한테 돈주는거 존나 아까워.

Fag
Homossaekki
호모새끼

> He's a perverted **fag**.
> *Jeo jeojilseurun **homossaekki**.*
> 저 저질스런 **호모새끼**.

Loner
Wangtta
왕따

Also known as *ijime* (이지메), the word used in Japan. In Korea, a loner (usually the weakest link) gets picked on by the entire class. This has become a huge social problem since several bullied loners have committed suicide. But you know what? It's not as bad as the Japanese *ijime*.

Police
Gyeongchal
경찰

Cops
Jjapsae
짭새

Gangsta
Jopok
조폭

> You **gangstas** think you are tough shit?
> *Jopok imyeon daya?*
> **조폭**이면 다야?

Millionaire
Buja
부자

> My **millionaire** sugar daddy buys me whatever I want!
> *Nae **buja** hogu ajeossi naega wonhaneungeo da sajo!*
> 내 **부자** 호구아저씨 내가 원하는거 다 사줘!

Broke-ass person
Gananbaengi
가난뱅이

> Quit being such a **broke ass**.
> *Ya, don eopneun **gananbaengi**jit geumanhae.*
> 야, 돈없는 **가난뱅이**짓 그만해.

Unemployed person
Baeksu / Baekjo
백수 / 백조

> Hey, aren't you partying too hard for an **unemployed person**?
> *Ya, **baeksu**rago neomu noneungeoanya?*
> 야, **백수**라고 너무 노는거 아냐?

Genius
Cheonjae
천재

> **Wow, you are a genius!**
> *Wuwa, neo jeongmal cheonjaeya!*
> 우와, 너 정말 **천재**야!

Princess
Gongju
공주

It's nice to be called a princess by your parents when you are five, but if you're still "Princess" when you're a teenager, you've got to admit that you're a conceited bitch.

> **You have a serious princess syndrome!**
> *Neo simhan gongjubyeongiya!*
> 너 심한 **공주병**이야!

Koreans think narcissistic spoiled brats like Paris Hilton are mentally ill, which makes the girls delusional about being a princess, hence "princess syndrome."

Prince
Wangja
왕자

On the flip side, *wangja* are conceited Korean boys who, in their minds, are perfect princes all the girls want. Wait, don't all the guys think that?

Average Joe
Pyeongbeomhan saram
평범한 사람

> **Don't try to stand out; being an average Joe is the best.**
> *Neomu twijimara, pyeongbeomhange choegoya.*
> 너무 튀지마라, **평범한게** 최고야.

Jesus freak
Yesujaengi
예수쟁이

> **Jesus freaks think they are married to God.**
> *Haneunnimgwa gyeolhonhan michin yesujaengideul.*
> 하느님과 결혼한 미친 **예수쟁이**들.

CHAPTER 3

PARTY KOREAN

HANGUKAESUH NOLTTAE HANEUNMAL

한국에서 놀때 하는말

●●●●●Let's party!
Uri nolja!
우리 놀자!

When it comes to partying, Koreans are the Irish of Asia. They even get all red-faced when they get drunk, which is often. Unlike in the States, though, Koreans don't just park it at one bar. They won't stop until they've gone to at least four places to drink *soju*, beer, makgeolli (Korean rice drink), wine and hard liquor. In fact, partying is such an integral part of Korean culture that you can't say you've truly experienced Korea until you've gotten drunk as shit off cheap *soju*, performed bad karaoke, then watched yourself on YouTube (thanks to your thoughtful friends) singing and dance to Korean songs you've never heard before.

Are you up for...
Junbi dwaennya...
준비 됐냐...

partying?
nol junbi dwaennya?
놀 준비 됐냐?

drinking?
sul masil junbi dwaennya?
술 마실 준비 됐냐?

going out?
nagal junbi dwaennya?
나갈 준비 됐냐?

getting wasted?
jugeul junbi dwaennya?
죽을 준비 됐냐?

Literally, "Are you ready to die?" Koreans don't stop drinking until they black out!

a drink?
hanjan hal junbi dwaennya?
한잔 할 준비 됐냐?

Bottom's up!
Won syat!
원샷!

Literally, "one shot," alluding to the fact that you don't get to sip *soju* in Korea. You drink all of it—or your Korean drinking buddies will push you until you learn to. So learn quick!

The first round / second round / third round
Ilcha / icha / samcha
일차 / 이차 / 삼차

In the U.S., the first, second and third rounds may be at the same bar, but in Korea each round takes place in a different drinking establishment. As they say in Korea, first is to eat and drink, second is to sing and drink more, and third is to drink even more.

Do you have a **plan**?
*Mo **halggeo** eopnya?*
뭐 **할거** 없냐?

Where are you headed?
Eodiga?
어디가?

Let's have a drink.
Sul hanjan haja.
술 한잔 하자.

Let's go for round 2.
*Uri **icha** gaja!*
우리 이차 가자!

Let's drink till the end!
*Uri hanbeon **kkeukkaji** gaboja!*
우리 한번 끝까지 가보자!

Let's drink till we die!
*Uri hanbeon **jugeo**boja.*
우리 한번 죽어보자.

Do you know any hot spots?
***Mul joeun got** ara?*
물 좋은 곳 알아?

Let's stay up all night!
*Uri **bamsaeja**!*
우리 밤새자!

Let's drink just one more bottle!
*Uri ttak **hanbyeongman deo** haja!*
우리 딱 한병만 더 하자!

Let's play **till the sunrise!**
Hae tteul ttaekkaji nolja!
해 뜰 때까지 놀자!

Cheers~
Geonbae~
건배~

> **Cheers** to a long and drunken night!
> *Geonbae! Uri jugeoboja!*
> 건배! 우리 죽어보자!

Cin cin!
Jjan!
짠!

> **Cin cin** to a bottomless glass!
> *Jjan haja!*
> 짠 하자!

Let's raise a glass.
Jan deulja.
잔 들자.

·····Where Koreans get down
Nolgeori
놀거리

Koreans don't just go on bar crawls. Oh no, they're far more determined about their drunken debauchery than that. After dinner (which itself will feature copious amounts of drinking), on a typical Korean night out, you'll hit up a plethora of bars for a spectacular evening of drunken imbibing before moving onward to a *noraebang*, or karaoke house, where you'll get even more plastered while performing slurred renditions of '80s pop hits. If you're still on your feet after that, you might cap things off at a club for yet more drinking or—if you need to sober up—the *jimjilbang*, a 24-hour sauna where you can leech all that delicious poison out of your body.

Bar

Suljip

술집

In areas like Hongdae, a district surrounding an artsy university, there are strips of bars catering to your every mood—fusion bars, traditional Korean bars, Westernized bars, Japanese bars and karaoke bars. If you don't like the joint you've meandered into, just pick up and move on to the next!

Karaoke house

Noraebang

노래방

Your voice might suck, but honestly, in Korea nobody gives a shit. Karaoke is something of a Korean national pastime, and it's always done in private rooms where you can butcher Journey songs with nobody but your friends around to make fun of you. And it only costs about $10 an hour to rent a room!

> **You sing well.**
> ***Norae*** *jom hane.*
> 노래 좀 하네.

Club

Club

클럽

Guys and girls from 18 to 30 go to the club to dance their asses off. (Well, dancing your ass off you can do at home in front of your mirror—I don't want to see any jiggly asses). If you are looking for a hot one-night stand, a drunken friend you won't remember the next day, or if you are just plain too drunk to care, there are great clubs all over. Note: Since techtonic is so hot in Korea, all the clubs will play similar music. Hongdae's filled with tons of options, but Itaewon's the place to go if you are looking for Korean girls ready to throw themselves at handsome foreigners. It's also the place to go to if you are sick of short yellow faces with straight black hair—all the foreigners hang out there. Gangnam's another good place to check out; it's also home to two well-known hip-hop clubs, Harlem and NB.

> **Are there any hot girls at the club?**
> ***Clube*** *mul joa?*
> 클럽에 물 좋아?

ID check / dress code check
Mul gwalli

뭄관리

Bouncers in Korea do an ID check and, more importantly, enforce a dress code. So you better look bangin' if you want to get in!

Nightclub
Night

나이트

The difference between nightclubs and clubs is a fat wallet. At clubs, guys can use charm and dance skills to hook up. But if men want to expend less energy on the game and have some Benjamins to throw around, they head to the nightclubs, typically referred to as "night." All the girls are hotties who get free admission and drinks because, well, they're hotties. Guys shell out a ridiculously high cover to enter and then they also get to pay for all the drinks inside. But all that green being thrown around means you get to stare at, talk to and/or dance with the pretty thangs all you want. You can even ask a waiter to bring your favorite girl to your table—without fear of a "no way, Jose."

Booking
Booking

부킹

This nightclub practice involves tipping waiters who will then escort women to men's tables, where chicks imbibe expensive drinks in exchange for their company. The crazy thing is that even though the babes know what's going on, the chosen women still put up a show of resistance, you know, for modesty's sake. While a female might "book" a guy, it's pretty rare (she'd probably be considered a ho, and therefore undesirable). Of course men do try to get the women drunk enough to leave the club for more intimate places. Wink, wink!

Club promoter
Bbikki

삐끼

Club promoters often approach you on the street with special offers or promotions.

Playground

Noriteo

놀이터

There are playgrounds in nearly every apartment complex in Korea and they often turn into gathering places for underage teenagers to get together and drink at night.

Rooftop

Oksang

옥상

Seoul is covered by tall apartment buildings. Most of them are over 25-floors tall; it's fun to sneak up to the rooftop of the building and party like a rock star above the city.

Sauna

Jjimjilbang

찜질방

Korean saunas, with partitioned bathhouses for men and women, are open 24/7. Normally used for family nights, saunas have different common areas to choose from: one room may have PCs or DVDs, another manicures or massages. You can even pick up a snack or sleep here—like if you are too drunk and broke to catch a cab home. It's only about $10 a night, and you'll even look pretty presentable the next day.

Playroom

Noribang

놀이방

Teenagers rent these common rooms at motels; each comes complete with a shower, a bed, and a PlayStation. It's a great place to meet up and chill. You can even throw a fabulous party here—just add balloons, ribbon, dresses and, of course, booze.

PC café
PC bang
ㅍ|ㅆ|방

A PC café provides some of the fastest Internet service in the world. Kids love to go here to play video games. You can even catch some gamers skipping school to play online games here. Fan of WoW? Check out the PC cafés.

Manga café
Manhwabang
만화방

These are like Korean libraries for people who like to dick off reading magazines and Manga instead of studying. You can smoke and eat in here, too.

Video room
Bidiobang
비디오방

These rooms with a couch and a TV are where underage students go to supposedly watch movies but really just end up having sex.

Wine bar
Wainba
와인바

Sophisticated white collar people (i.e., pretentious jerks) like to eat at these elegant wine bars. Take your girlfriend to a glamorous wine bar with eye-poppingly high prices, and she just might give you what you've been waiting for.

Hof
Hopeu
호프

This is a bar/restaurant geared toward drinking and eating. This is from the German word *hoff* meaning a "place."

Trailer bar
Pojangmacha
포장마차

Trailers are typically outdoor tents on wheels that provide street food like chicken feet and *soju*. These places are usually open until 4 or 5 in the morning, and they're where Koreans without a lot of money go to get drunk and talk to friends.

·····Totally wasted
Sul chwiham
술 취함

Koreans don't fuck around when it comes to getting their drink on. Getting plastered is an art in Korea, and certain customs must be followed. For instance, it's traditional that someone else at the table pours your drink (and you theirs)— it's a gesture of respect and friendship. If you do it yourself, you're rejecting this. So be sure to keep a steady supply of friends on hand, because unless you're a pussy lightweight, you're gonna need a lot of drinks poured your way.

Holy shit, I'm...
Ssibal, na...
씨발, 나...

a little tipsy.
jom eojireowo.
좀 어지러워.

smashed.
gondeurae mandeurae.
곤드래 만드래.

trashed.
manchwi.
만취.

plastered.
kkoratda.
꼴았다.

hammered.
Kkwaladwaetda.
꽉라댔다.

I am buzzed!
Na chwihaneungeo gata!
나 취하는거 같아!

FAMOUS DISTRICTS IN SEOUL)))
YUMYEONGHAN GOT
유명한 곳

Hongdae
홍대

The Hongdae district is known for its clubs and for creative types selling their homemade jewelry on the street (read: Korean hippies). It's kinda like Korea's version of Berkeley with more clubs and bars. (Can you imagine that?)

Apgujeong
압구정

Home to many celebrities, Apgujeong is the Beverly Hills of Korea. It's great if you like shopping centers and overpriced cafés.

Myeongdong
명동

This famous area features huge malls with cheap goods as well as some street shops great for exploring. It's where most Japanese tourists come to buy stuff so if you are a shopper, you have to check it out. But if you're looking for brand names and high quality, you're in the wrong place—Koreans are known for producing brand imitations and this venue showcases many of these knockoffs.

Men aren't supposed to use the word "drunk" in Korea. So even if you are, just act like everything is fine and pretend you can hold your liquor.

I blacked out last night.
Na eoje pileum kkeunkkyeosseosseo.
나 어제 **필름 끊겼었어**.

I am about to throw up.
Na ssollyeo.
나 **쏠려**.

I'm gonna hurl.
Na ssonneunda.
나 **쏜는다**.

Insadong
인사동

Insadong features traditional Korean shopping centers where you can buy souvenirs and other touristy crap for your family and friends. They also have a lot of old-fashioned teahouses where you can experience authentic Korean tea, if you need somewhere to bring your parents or someone you're trying to impress.

Yeouido
여의도

Seoul's business and administrative center, Yeouido has plentiful public parks that attract weekend bicyclists and bladers. And the views of the country's famous Han River are spectacular.

Olympic park
Olympic gongwon
올림픽 공원

The stadium and surrounding park were built for the 1988 Summer Olympics. On weekends, families and friends come out here to picnic and bike.

North gate / East gate
Namdaemun / Dongdaemun
남대문 / 동대문

These gates mark Seoul's original borders. Now there are 24-hour shopping districts here. Isn't modernization great?

I have to vomit.
Na to haeyahae.
나 토 해야해.

I just blew chunks everywhere.
Na jigeum bburyeosseo.
나 지금 뿌렸어.

You are slurring.
Nu hyeo kkoinda.
너 혀 꼬인다.

·····Booze

Sul

술

In Korea, you never refuse a drink poured by an elder (you know, that whole age-hierarchy thing again). So if you're partying with older friends, you may be in for a rough night. Hopefully they'll take pity on you and stop pouring your drinks before you end up taking a transvestite to a love motel. But if they don't, at least you'll have a funny story to tell the next day. That, and lots and lots of shame.

Gimme a …
… juseyo.
… 주세요.

soju.
Soju
소주

The ubiquitous *soju*, traditionally made with rice, is Korea's answer to vodka. It's cheap and will get you fucked up. A lot of celebrities shell out big money for special *soju* brands, but they're all just basically watered-down versions of American vodka.

Order me another yogurt soju—I haven't passed out yet.
Ya, yogut soju hanbyung duh cikyuh! Na a-jig jungsin maljjanghae.
야, 요구르트 소주 한병 더 시켜! 나 아직 정신 말짱해.

unfiltered rice wine.
Makgeolli / Takju
막걸리 / 탁주

A cloudy concoction that's historically been a farmer's drink, this Korean sake has just recently become en vogue with the younger generation. It's cheap, sweet and best served with *buchimgae*, Korean pancakes.

beer.
Maekju

맥주

Popular Korean beers include Hite and OB. Drink it cold with Korean fried chicken and you're in business!

liquor.
Yangju

양주

A term that describes any drink coming from the west: wine, brandy, whiskey, vodka, etc.

Korean sake.
Jeongjong

정종

Korean medicine drink.
Baekseju

백세주

Baekseju is actually a brand of *soju* made for girls who can't tolerate the smell and taste of "regular" *soju*. This sweet drink, flavored with ginseng, is actually good for you if you limit your drinking to a bottle or less (like that ever happens).

> ### Eunjug Kim's such a lightweight, she only drinks Korean medicine drink.
> *Kim Eun-jung eun neomu swipge chwihanda.*
> ***Baekseju**man masine.*
>
> 김은정은 너무 쉽게 취한다. 백세주만 마시네.

raspberry drink.
Bokbunja

복분자

This tends to be popular with the ladies due to its sweetness. It's also supposedly viagra-in-a-bottle for guys (but if you drink too much of it, you'll be too shit faced to get it up, so take your chances).

·····Drinking games
Sul game
술 게임

These games are extremely popular in Korea. They're like beer pong, but they're done at a bar and usually played sitting down.

The Game of Death
Deo game ob desseu
더 게임어브 데트
A group will often start out with this game to get each other drunk fast. It's pretty much a no-brainer: You chant "the game of death" and point at someone you'd like to see drunk. The one with most fingers pointed at has to drink. It's crude but effective at getting everyone fucked up.

Titanic (aka, Sake Bomb)
Titanic
타이타닉
This is like a sake bomb (with *soju* instead). But you don't just make a *soju* bomb (*poktanju*) and down it—all drinkers participate in creating the Titanic. First, pour half a glass of beer. Then put an empty *soju* glass inside the glass of beer. People then take turns pouring as much *soju* as they want into the beer glass. The person who sinks the *soju* glass has to drink the whole thing. Bottom's up!

Black Rose
Heukjangmi
흑장미
The exact opposite of the Black Night, this is when a man finds a woman to take a shot for him in a drinking game. But if she refuses, he has to take double shots.

King Game
King game
킹게임
Gather chopsticks (yes, Koreans eat with chopsticks, so you would have them) equal to the number of participants (e.g., five

players = five chopsticks). Put the letter "K" (for "King") on one chopstick then number the remaining chopsticks, starting with 1. Each person then picks a chopstick. The person with the K-chopstick can make the others do whatever he or she wants. For example, the king can make number 1 and 4 kiss each other. If you are both dudes, well, enjoy the hot breath.

Black Knight
Heukgisa
흑기사
This is when a woman finds a man to take a shot for her while playing a drinking game. The girl normally has to do a favor for him afterward (sexual or otherwise).

3, 6, 9
Sam yuk gu
삼육구
Everyone goes around counting up from 1. You clap on every number that contains 3, 6, and 9. If you fail to clap or say your number, you chug.

The Baskin Robbins 31
Baskin Robbins Sseotiwon
베스킨 로빈스 써리원
Someone starts counting from 1, and the next person continues counting, in order, saying either 1, 2 or 3 numbers per turn. So if you begin by saying "1" the next player can say "2," "2, 3" or "2, 3, 4." The person who gets to 31 has to drink.

·····Taking it easy today
Oneureun swillae
오늘은 쉴래

Your liver can only take so much abuse before it goes into revolt. So when you've had enough and can't take another night of hard living at the *noraebang*, try some of these phrases out on your new friends and then prepare yourself to be called several iterations of the word "pussy."

I am dying from a hangover.
Sukchi ttaemune jugeulkkeo gata.
숙취 때문에 죽을꺼 같아.

I'm still drunk from last night.
Eoje masin sule ajikdo chwihesseo.
어제 마신 술에 **아직도 취**했어.

I think I have cirrhosis.
Na ganyeom inneungeo gata.
나 **간염**있는것 같아.

It's too much, count me out.
Oneureun bbaejo, na himdeureo.
오늘은 **빼줘**, 나 힘들어.

Pass.
Oneureun pass.
오늘은 **패스**.

See you next time.
Da-eume boja.
다음에 보자.

I need to go home early.
Na jibe iljjik gabwaya dwae.
나 집에 **일찍** 가봐야 돼.

My curfew is 10.
Tongeumi yeolsiya.
통금이 *10*시야.

I'm just gonna chill tonight.
Nan oneul geunyang swillae.
난 오늘 그냥 **쉴래**.

I'm a bed-wetting little girl and I can't handle my liquor.
Na aegiraseo sul mot masyeo.
나 애기라서 **술 못 마셔**.

·····Drugs
Mayak
마약

Unlike in America where there's a pill for everything, Korean culture isn't big on drugs, recreational or otherwise. Even over-the-counter medications like pain relievers aren't widely used. That's not to say that nobody does drugs in Korea. It's just not a mainstream thing that you hear talked about a lot.

Have you ever tried **drugs**?
*Neo **mayak** haebwasseo?*
너 **마약** 해봤어?

Weed
Daemacho
대마초

Although weed is generally a pretty harmless drug and treated as such in most of the world, in Korea it falls under into the same category as hard drugs like cocaine and heroin, and the cops treat it all the same. That's right, a measly little joint could add up to serious jail time—so toke at your own risk.

Where can I get some **weed**?
***Daemacho** eodiseo guhalsu isseo?*
대마초 어디서 구할수 있어?

Pot
Tteol
떡

Pothead
Tteoljaengi
떡쟁이

Most hard drugs get imported into the country through foreigners or Korean students who study abroad. So college parties would likely be your best bet if you're looking for a hookup.

CiGARETTES)))
DAMBAE
담배

Cigarettes are very popular in Korea. Not surprising, since every other drug is so hard to get. And at just $2 a pack, how can you not smoke them? Korean cigs are not as toxic as the usual U.S. brands (like Marlboro), probably because most of the brands are charcoal-filtered. There are TONS of different brands in Korea but these are a few of the most popular that are widely available:

This
Dis
디스
Kids love This because of its chic design and smooth taste.

Raison
Rejong
레종
Another youth favorite, especially with first-time smokers who wanna fit in with other smokers.

Esse
Esse
에세
These affordable slim sticks are popular with women.

88
Palpal
팔팔
An old standby, 88 is one of the original cigarette brands in Korea. Most of the older generation smokes this high-octane, addictive cig—what doesn't kill you will make you stronger.

Time
Time
타임
This is another long-time ciggy favored by OGs—longevity in the market goes a long way when it comes to brand loyalty.

Heroin
Heroin
헤로인

Horse (heroin)
Hirobbong
히로뽕

> **Why is she acting like she's on the horse?**
> *Jeonyeon wae **hirobbong** han haengdongeul hanya?*
> 저년 왜 **히로뽕** 한 행동을 하냐?

Coke
Cokein
코케인

Crack
Matgannom / Matgannyeon
맛간놈 / 맛간년

> **That girl ain't nothing but a crackhead.**
> *Jeonyeon wanjeon **matgannyeon**ine.*
> 저년 완전 **맛간년**이네.

Ecstasy
Exteossi
엑스터시

You can get this at a lot of clubs in urban areas if you know the right person.

Addiction
Jungdok
중독

Addict
Jungdokja
중독자

> **Can you be addicted to weed?**
> *Daemachoe **jungdok** dwelsu isseo?*
> 대마초에 **중독**될 수 있어?

Junky
Mayakjaengi / Yakjaengi
마약쟁이 / 약쟁이

Some junky just offered to **suck my dick** for crack.
*Eotteon **yakjaengi**ga jigeum mayak jumyeon **oral** haejugetde.*
어떤 **약쟁이**가 지금 마약 주면 **오랄** 해주겠데.

Korean Crazy Glue
Bbondeu
본드

Since illegal substances are hard to obtain, Koreans love to get high off of everyday items that you can get from hardware stores, such as crazy glue and butane gas.

Do you want to get high with crazy glue?
*Bbondeu bbalgo **bbyong galkka**?*
본드빨고 **뿅 갈까**?

I huffed some glue.
*Bbondeu **bbarasseo**.*
본드 **빨았어**.

Butane gas
Butan gas
부탄가스

I went crazy after **huffing** butane gas.
*Butan gas **masigo** dorasseo.*
부탄가스 **마시고** 돌았어.

CHAPTER 4

BODY KOREAN
HANGUKESEO WOEMOE GWANHAE YAEGIHANEUN MAL
한국에서 외모에 관해 애기하는 말

•••••The Korean ideal
Hanguk minam mi-in
한국 미남 미인

Koreans are increasingly adopting Western ideals of beauty. They want to be taller and skinnier, possess a higher and pointier nose, and have whiter skin. In fact, Westerners are big hits in Korea. So if you're striking out in the good ol' U.S. of A. because you're not "exotic looking" enough, you might be a home run in Korea. But if you're hoping to find a Korean who will love you for your inner beauty, wake up. Koreans are very superficial. So superficial, in fact, that the nation ranks number one in plastic surgery per capita.

As mentioned above, Koreans want to look more Western. Korean men want to look like Michelangelo's statue of David and women want to be Venus. So naturally, Koreans all want different eyes, noses, mouths and ears than they already have.

Facial features
Imokgubi
이목구비

He has **striking features.**
*Geueui eolgureun **imokgubiga ttoryeothae**.*
그의 얼굴은 **이목구비가 또렷해**.

He / She is...
Geuneun / Geunyeoneun...
그는... / 그녀는...

cute.
gwiyeopda.
귀엽다.

pretty.
yaebbeuda.
예쁘다.

beautiful.
areumdapda.
아름답다.

sexy.
sseksihada.
섹시하다.

good looking. (men)
minamida.
미남이다.

good looking. (women)
minyeoida.
미녀이다.

popular.
ingiga jota.
인기가 좋다.

skinny.
mallatda.
말랐다.

tall.
kigakeuda.
키가크다.

ripped. (too muscular)
urakburak hada.
우락부락 하다.
This has a negative connotation in Korean.

buff.
tantanhada.
탄탄하다.

voluptuous.
jjukjjuk bbangbbang hada.
쭉쭉빵빵 하다.

handsome.
jal saengyeotda.
잘 생겼다.

metrosexual.
kkonminam i da.
꽃미남이다.
Literally, "flowerly handsome." Many Korean women fantasize about their men being pretty and having girly faces. It's common to see popular male singers dressed up and wearing makeup like women.

He / She is a...
Geuneun / Geunyeoneun …ida.
그는 / 그녀는 ... 이다.

natural beauty.
jayeon mi-in
자연 미인

plastic surgery beauty.
seonghyeong mi-in
성형 미인

multi-talented beauty.
palbangmi-in
판방미인

This term refers to someone who is talented in many areas and beautiful. You know, those people you want to hate but you can't because they're also nice and gentle. Well, Koreans have a nice word for those nice people. I personally hate them.

pole.
jeonbotdae
전봇대

string bean.
kkeokdari
꺽다리

A person so tall that they can be bent and still be tall.

fat ass.
ttungttaengi
뚱땡이

wild, sexy man.
yaseongnam
야성남

Though the metrosexual look is popular, the manly man look has been gaining steam thanks to a recent spate of seminude celebrities showing off their buff guns on TV.

He / She has…
Geuneun / Geunyeoneun…gajigoitda.
그는 / 그녀는 … 가지고 있다.

a small face.
jageun eolgul
작은 얼굴을

a beautiful face.
eoljjang
얼짱

Literally, "face number one" or "face the best." *Eol* (얼) is shorthand for *eolgul* (얼굴; face) while *jjang* (짱) means "number one" or "the best." You say, "she is the best face" *guenye nuen eoljjang i da* (그녀는 얼짱이다).

a beautiful nose bridge.

ottokhan koreul

오똑한 코를

Have you seen any genetics-defying high and pointy noses on Korean friends you have in the U.S.? Korean noses are usually very small and flat, so if you see a straight nose bridge leading up to a pointy nose tip (longer than 2 cm), it tells you one of two things: Either he or she is really lucky, or it's a beautiful product of the knife. The procedures are expensive, so don't throw balls around these surgically altered schnozes.

big eyes.

keun nuneul

큰 눈을

long legs.

long darireul

롱 다리를

a great body. (same as voluptuous)

esseu line-eul

에스 라인을

an awesome body.

momjjang

몸짱

This is another word better used as "he is an awesome body." Say *geuneun momjjangida* (그는 몸짱이다) instead. The other way just sounds cheesy anyways.

a killer body.

aju jugineun momeul

아주 죽이는 몸을

big guns.

tantanhan pareul

딴딴한 팔을

washboard abs.

chocolate baereul

초콜렛 배를

This is when a guy has six pack that resembles a Hershey's chocolate bar.

PLASTIC SURGERY)))
SUNGHYEONG SUSUL
성형 수술

Plastic surgery is really popular in Korea. It was considered shameful when people first started getting it done back in the '80s, but today it's a lot more acceptable and people are pretty open about their surgeries. This cosmetic boom was driven by widespread superficiality in a country with top-quality surgeons charging very affordable prices. But all this surgery is starting to have some very creepy results now that many celebrities are starting to become indistinguishable from one another.

Eyelid surgery
Ssangkapul susul
쌍까풀 수술
This surgery is the most common procedure Koreans try to look more "Western."

Nose job
Ko susul
코 수술

Boob job
Gaseum susul
가슴 수술

Lipo
Jibang heubipsul
지방흡입술

Botox
Botocs / jureum jegeo
보톡스 / 주름 제거

Did you go **under the knife**?
Neo eolgure kal dennya?
너 얼굴에 칼댔나?
There's a really gnarly video on YouTube of a Korean woman who got obsessed with plastic surgery and injected sesame oils into her face. It's gross. Check it out.

honey thighs.
kkulbeokjireul
꿀벅지를

a six pack.
sixpaekeul
씩스팩을

•••••The Korean ugly
Hangook poktan
한국 폭탄

In general, Koreans are a pretty sexy group of people. And if you had to choose just one nationality to sleep with for the rest of your life, you could do a lot worse than to choose Koreans. But despite the overall attractiveness of its people, Korea does harbor a few outliers. And by "outliers" I mean butt-ugly fatties that should never, ever reproduce.

He / She is…
Geuneun… / Geunyeoneun…
그는… / 그녀는…

unattractive.
mot saengyeotda.
못생겼다.

fugly.
maejuda.
매주다.
Literally, "fermented beans."

busted.
poktanida.
폭탄이다.
Literally, "bomb."

butt ugly.
hobakida.
호박이다.
Literally, "pumpkin."

too skinny.
bbijjeok mallatda.
삐쩍 말랐다.

anorexic.
angsanghage mallatda.
앙상하게 말랐다.

bony.
bbyeo bakke eopda.
뼈 밖에 없다.

unpopular.
ingiga eopda.
인기가 없다.

You are…
Neoneun…
너는...

an ugly man.
chunamida.
추남이다.

an ugly woman.
chunyeoda.
추녀다.

a fat boy. / a fat girl.
ttungboda. / ttungnyeoda.
뚱보다. / 뚱녀다.

a pig.
dwaejida.
돼지다.

a dwarf.
nanjaengida. / lujeoda.
난쟁이다. / 루저다.

On a popular show in Korea called Minyeodeului Suda, a
female university student labeled any guys under 5' 6" losers.
Korean men were outraged! But the term stuck and now all
short men are called losers in Korea.

a fatso.
ttungttaengida.
뚱땡이다.

chubbier.
salijjeotda.
살이쪘다.

He / She has...
Geuneun / Geunyeoneun ... gajigo itda.
그는 / 그녀는...가지고 있다.

a big head. (applies to men)
keun daegarireul
큰 대가리를

a big face.
keun eolrgureul
큰 얼굴을

small eyes.
jageun nuneul
작은 눈을

a gut.
ttongbaereul
똥배를

a muffintop.
tubeu-reul ggyeosseo
튜브를 꼈어
Literally, "wearing inner tube around your waist."

short legs.
shot dari / jangnong dari
쏫 다리 / 장롱 다리

fat legs.
mudarireul
무다리를
Literally, "radish legs."

uneven ass cheeks.
jjak gungdaengireul
짝 궁댕이를

a fat ass.
ori gungdaengireul
오리 궁댕이를
Literally, "duck ass."

a saggy ass.
cheojin eongdeongireul
처진 엉덩이를

MORE UGLY KOREAN)))

Here are some popular Korean sayings to make fun of others' appearances:

You are **small like a booger**!
Ko ttakji manhange kkabulgo isseo!
코 딱지 만한게 까불고 있어!

You are **small like a RAT**!
Jwisaekki manhange kkabulgo isseo!
쥐새끼 만한게 까불고 있어!

You are **a size of shit bag of a dwarf**.
Nanjaengi ttongjaru manhange kkabulgo isseo!
난쟁이 똥자루 만한게 까불고 있어!

Who looks at the ugly?
Nuga jeogeo bondago?
누가 저거 본다고?

Pearl necklace on pig's neck!
Dwaejimoge jinju mokgeori!
돼지목에 진주 목걸이.

You can't put lipstick on a **pig**.
Hobage jul geutneundago subak dwaenya?
호박에 줄 긋는다고 수박돼냐?

Literally, "Can pumpkins become watermelons with lines?" Koreans consider pumpkins ugly but watermelons handsome. So even if an ugly person puts on beautiful clothes, lots of makeup and expensive, brand-name accessories, he or she will never be beautiful. At least, that's what they used to say, but if you spend your life savings on multiple plastic surgeries, you might just be able to get prettier.

Your legs are **as short as a dresser's**!
*Neo wanjeon **jangnong dariya**!*
너 다리 완전 장롱 다리야!

If you bend over and look at the bottom of your dresser, you can see how small the space in between the ground and the dresser is, because most dressers have short legs.

Holy shit, your head is the size of a watermelon!
Uwa, jenjang neo meoriga wanjeon subagiya!
우와, 젠장, 너 머리가 완전 수박이야!
Korean watermelons are smaller than the ginormous fruits you see in U.S. supermarkets—they're about as big as jack-o-lantern pumpkins.

You have radish legs!
Neo wanjeon mudariya!
너 완전 무다리야!
One of most popular sayings used to insult girls with short, fat legs.

·····Piss
Ojum
오줌

Korea doesn't have many public restrooms. Lots of restaurants and bars share bathrooms and require a key to get in. Because of the scarcity of public johns, it's tough to find a nice place to pop a squat. So you better learn the phrases below to show how bad you gotta use it!

Where's the can?
Hwajangsiri eodiyeyo?
화장실이 어디예요?

I need to piss bad!
Ojum maryeo!
오줌 마려!

I
Na …
나…

> **gotta pee.**
> *ojum ssayahae.*
> 오줌 싸야해.

gotta **piss.**
swi ssayahae.
쉬 싸야해.

gotta **take a leak**
mul bbaeyahae.
물 빼야해.

Can you pass me some TP?
Hyuji jom gatda jullae?
휴지 좀 갖다 줄래?
There are sometimes vending machines outside of public restrooms to provide toiletries.

Shit, I missed the mark and pissed all over my hands.
*A sipal, jojun jal motaeseo sone **ojum da mudeosseo.***
아 시팔, 조준 잘 못해서 손에 오줌 다 묻었어.
It's common to witness public urination at night when men are shit-faced drunk on the sidewalk.

My bladder is about to explode!
Ojumbbo teojilgeo gata!
오줌보 터질거 같아!

Are you going number 1 or number 2?
Neo keungeo jageungeo?
너 큰거 작은거?
Literally, "Are you going big or small?"

·····Shit
Ttong
똥

You may be surprised to find that many public restrooms in modern Korea still sport the old-fashioned seatless bowl. This means you'll be doing the Asian squat a lot, so hope to God that your quad strength doesn't give out. Oh yeah, and don't forget to carry a pack of tissue with you just in case, since a lot of restrooms don't provide TP.

SHiTTY SAYiNGS)))
TTONGMAL
똥말

It seems like every culture has its own sayings about shit that would confuse the hell out of foreigners. For instance, what would a F.O.B. Korean think if you told him that he was "full of shit" or that his haircut was "the shit"? It's no different in Korea, where they have their own special phrases. So keep your ears peeled for these little colloquial nuggets.

The dog speared in shit criticizes the dog speared in foliage.
Ttong mudeun gaega gyeo mudeun gaebogo mora handa.
똥묻은 개가 겨묻은 개보고 뭐라한다.

Na ttong bbujijik bbujijik ssasseo.
나 똥 뿌지직 뿌지직 쌌어.
There's no good translation for this since it's simply the onomatopoeic sound of shit coming out of your butthole. Saying it basically means that you just took a shit.

You are the shit, your shit is the thickest!
Neo jalnasseo, ne ttong gulgeo!
너 잘났어, 네 똥 굵어!
This is a mocking and sarcastic backhanded compliment.

I can't eat anymore; my stomach is full of **shit**.
*Deoisang mot meogeo, nae baega **ttong**euro chasseo.*
더이상 못 먹어, 내 배가 **똥**으로 찼어.
This one pretty much speaks for itself.

Feces
Daebyeon
대변

Poop
Eunga
응가

Do you want to go poo poo?
***Eunga** halkka?*
응가 할까?
Mothers often say to their babies, "Let's poo poo together!"

I am about to shit in my pants.
Bajie ttong ssalgeot gata.
바지에 똥 쌀것 같아.

I have to take a...
Na ... ssayahae.
나 ... 싸야해.

> **dump.**
> *han mudeogi*
> 한무더기

> **shit.**
> *ttong*
> 똥

I have diarrhea.
Na seolssahae.
나 설사해.

Blended shit (half rhea, half solid)
Garaseo mandeun ttong
갈아서 만든 똥

·····Fart / Burp
Bangu / Teureum
방구 / 트름

By American standards, it's considered rude to fart or burp in public, but for Koreans it's just a natural bodily occurrence. (Well, at least burping is; farting is still kinda frowned upon.) So don't look surprised when the elderly Korean gentleman in the booth next to you belches kimchi in your face.

Who farted?
Bangu nuga ggyeosseo?
방구 누가 꼈어?

That stinks.
Naemsae juginda.
냄새 죽인다.

Your ass is playing the flute!
Eongdeong-iga pirireul bune!
엉덩이가 피리를 부네!

Smells like a rotten egg.
Sseogeun dalgyal naemsaena.
썩은 닭걀 냄새나.

Your fart smells like old rotten kimchi.
Ni bangu orae mugeun kimchi naemsaena.
니 방구 오래 묵은 김치 냄새 나.

Burp
Teureum
트름

It's not considered rude by elders to burp at restaurants in Korea. However, if you're a youngster, you better keep your skills under wraps until you're with your friends.

Don't burp in front of me, you nasty shit.
Tereum hajima, deoreowun saekki.
트름하지마 더러운 새끼.

Hiccups
Ttalkkukjil
딱꾹질

Boogers
Kottakji
코딱지

"Boogers" in Korean is a combination of the words "nose" and "scalp."

Quit picking your boogers.
Kottakji jom geuman pa.
코딱지 좀 그만 파.

Snot
Konmul
콧물

> Wipe the **snot** off your face.
> *Konmul jom dagga.*
> **콧물** 좀 닦아.

Blow your nose.
Ko jom pureo.
코 좀 풀어.

Eye boogers
Nunkkop
눈꼽

> You have **eye boogers**!
> *Neo **nunkkop** kkyeosseo!*
> 너 **눈꼽**꼈어!

Earwax
Gwiji / Gwitbab
귀지 / 귓밥

> **Gwijigae** are good for taking out your earwax.
> ***Gwijigae**ro gwiji paneunge joa.*
> **귀지개**로 귀지 파는게 좋아.
>
> *Gwijigae* is a tool that's either made out of wood or metal; it
> resembles a long, thin spoon that's used to clean out your
> earwax.

·····Sickness
Byeong
병

I am not feeling well.
Momi anjoa.
몸이 안좋아.

I am sick.
Na apeo.
나 아퍼.

I'm hurt.
Na dacheossep.
나 다쳤어.

I am going to die.
Na jugeul geo gata.
나 죽을 거 같아.
Not literally—this is hyperbole expressing intense illness.

I think I caught a cold.
Gamgi geollin geo gata.
감기 걸린 거 같아.

Are you okay?
Neo gwenchana?
너 괜찮아?

Where does it hurt?
Eodi apeo?
어디 아퍼?

You don't look too hot.
Byeollo an joa boyeo.
별로 안 좋아 보여.

You are pale.
Eolguri changbaekhae.
얼굴이 창백해.

I have a stomachache.
Na baeapeo.
나 배아퍼.

I'm having my period.
Na saengrijungiya.
나 생리중이야.

I'm on the rag.
Geunariya.
그 날이야.

I have raging PMS.
Na saengri jeonira piemesseuro jirariya.
나 생리전이라 **피엠에스**로 지랄이야.

I have a fever.
Yeolna.
열나.

Call 119.
Ililgue jeonhwahae.
일일구에 전화해.
In Korea, 119 is what you call for the fire department.

·····Pharmacy
Yakguk
약국

Koreans practice a lot of Eastern medicine, but it's pretty easy to find more Westernized treatment and get the meds that you're used to.

Where are you hurting?
Eodiga apeoyo?
어디가 아퍼요?

Can you give me some headache medicine?
Geborin juseyo?
게보린 주세요?
This is basically Tylenol (acetaminophen).

Aspirin
Aspirin
아스피린

Ibuprofen
Ebupropen
이부프로펜

Cold medicine
Gamgiyak
감기약 (brand—판프린 에프)

Bug bite medicine
Mogiyak
모기약 (파스 —for mosquito bites)
This is hydrocortisone.

Tums
Baetalyak
배탈약 (brand—훼스탄)

Laxative
Seolsayak
설사약 (brand—정로환)

Red Bull
Bakaseu
박카스

Band-Aids
Banchango
반창고

Neosporin
Madekasol, husidin
마데카솔, 후시딘

Chinese herbal medicine ball
Wuhwangcheongsimwon
우황 청신원

This curative is made out of a bunch of Chinese herbs rolled into a small ball. It stinks like hell but cures you instantly when you are in mental or physical shock.

> **I'm in shock! I need Chinese medicine ball!**
> *Na nollasseo! Wuhwang cheongsimwon pilyohae!*
> 나 놀랐어! 우황청신원 픽요해!

CHAPTER 5

HORNY KOREAN

HANGUKESEO SSEUNEUN YAHANMAL

한국에서 쓰는 야한말

·····Sex
Sex / Sungwangye
섹스 / 성관계

Like most people, Koreans have getting laid on their minds 24/7. Talking openly about sex, however, is a different story. It's still pretty taboo there. And when it does happen, it's usually as an embarrassed euphemism or in English, because talking dirty just comes more naturally in fucking English.

Thanks to the Internet (i.e., porn), lots of new sexual terms are starting to flood the language. So your Korean friends will probably understand you now when you start to explain your *bukkake* fetish. But what are Koreans to do with this newfound sexual awakening? Most Koreans live with their parents until

they tie the knot, so bringing home a booty call to try out their new reverse-blumpkin moves is out of the question.

That's where the "love motel" (러브 모텔) comes in. These rendezvous points may sound sleazy to Westerners but are a fact of life for unmarried Asians. Here, you can fuck without having to worry about Mom or Dad walking in and seeing you punching mochi all night long. Surprisingly, the motels are often chic and well decorated, and they only cost about $40 to $50 per day. But for some reason, most people just use them for a couple hours, re-creating all the poses they see from the FREE in-room porn.

> **I want to sleep with you.**
> *Na neorang **jagosipeo**.*
> 나 너랑 **자고싶어**.

> **I want to do it with you.**
> *Na neorang **hagosipeo**.*
> 나 너랑 **하고싶어**.

I'm getting in the mood to...
Na ... hagosipeo.
나 ... 하고싶어.

> **make love.**
> *sarangeul nanugo*
> 사랑을 나누고

> **fuck.**
> *kong kkago*
> 콩 까고

•••••Cocks
Geosigi
거시기

Whoever said "It's not the size of the boat but the motion of the ocean" was full of shit. Bigger is better. Less is not more. And because a big Johnson is so important, there are lots of ways to describe one.

Penis
Mulgeon
물건

> **My penis is thicker than yours.**
> *Nae mulgeon-i nikkeoboda deo gulgeo.*
> 내 물건이 니꺼보다 더 굵어.

Baby penis
Gochu
고추

This term is used when adults comment on a baby boy's penis, a frequent occurrence in Korea since it's very popular to take young boys to public bathhouses.

> **Your baby penis is very handsome.**
> *I nomeui jasik **gochu** cham jal saengyeotnae.*
> 이 놈의 자식, **고추** 참 잘 생겼네.

Foreskin
Kkeopjil
껍질

> **Did you remove your foreskin?**
> *Neo jaji **kkeopjjil** kkannya?*
> 너 자지 **껍질** 깠냐?

Circumcise
Pogyeong susul
포경수술

> **to hunt whales**
> *goraejabi*
> 고래잡이
>
> This euphemism comes from coincidental homonyms:
> *pogyeong susul* (to circumcise) and *pogyeong-up* (whaling).

Can I lick your… ?
… haltado doe?
… 핥아도 뒈?

Can I spank your…?
… chyeodo doe?
… 쳐도 뒈?

Can I suck your…?
… bbarado doe?
… 빤아도 뒈?

Can I take a picture of your…?
… geogi sajin jjigeodo doe?
… 거기 사진 찍어도 뒈?

Don't touch my…
… manjijjima.
… 만지지마.

I love…
… na joahae.
… 나 좋아해.

Wow, that is one fantastic…
Uwa, … geugeo jeongmal juginda.
우와, … 그거 정말 죽인다.

I've never seen a … like that.
Hanbeondo … bonjeogi eopsseo.
한번도 ... 본적이 없어.

> **cock**
> *jaji*
> 자지

> **johnson**
> *namgeun*
> 남근

> **dick**
> *eumkyeong*
> 음경

> **wiener**
> *jot*
> 좆

> **erection**
> *balttak seon jaji*
> 발딱 선 자지

> **boner**
> *ttakttakhan jaji*
> 딱딱한 자지

> **head**
> *guidu*
> 귀두

> **nuts**
> *gohwan*
> 고환

> **nads**
> *eumnang*
> 음낭

> **balls**
> *bural*
> 불알

rim of the head
jaji kkeut
자지 끝

pubes (male)
jaji teol
자지 털

·····Tits and ass
Gaseumirang eongdeongi
가슴이랑 엉덩이

Tits, boobies, knockers, melons, breasts, tatas and fun bags. No matter what you call them, they're awesome. More awesome than a sweet ass, though? That's a debate that philosophers have long argued but never settled. But can't we all agree that both are magical in their own special way? From my girlfriends' experiences (and mine…can't deny it), we've come up with the following tendencies: American boys go for the asses when they kiss girls, and Korean boys, as awkward as the position can be, go for the boobies as they kiss girls. God damn mama's boys!

I love big…
Nan keun …ga joa.
난 큰 ... 가 좋아.

Can I squeeze your…?
Ne … jumul-leodo dwae?
네 ... 주물러도 돼?

Fondle my…
Nae … manjeojo.
내 ... 만져줘.

Pinch my…
…kkojibeojo.
...꼬집어줘.

Show me your...
... boyeohjobwa.
...보여줘봐.

breasts.
yubang
유방

tits.
gaseum
가슴

nipples.
jeotkkokji
젖꼭지

nips.
yudu
유두

ass.
eongdeongi
엉덩이

asshole.
ttonkkumeong
똥구멍

anus.
hangmun
항문

perineum.
hoe-eum
허음

·····Pussy time!
Boji sigan!
보지 시간!

Though they may be "all pink on the inside," there remains a plethora of terms to describe the female vajajay.

I want to lick your...
Na neo ... halko sipeo.
나 너 ... 핥고싶어.

Eat my...
Nae ... meogeojwo.
내 ... 먹어줘.

Fingerbang my...
Nae ... soneuro bagajo.
내 ... 손으로 박아줘.

I'm going to ravage your...
Naega ni ... mangateurilkkeoya..
내가 니 ... 망가뜨릴꺼야.

pussy.
boji
보지

cunt.
jil
질

hairy pussy.
teol maneun boji
털많은 보지

Don't expect to see Brazilians when you hook up with chicks in Korea. Here, hairy pussy is the norm.

shaved pussy.
baekboji
백보지

Literally, "blank pussy."

clitoris.
eumhaek
음핵

clit.
clitoris
크리토리스

love button.
kong
콩

Literally, "bean." Losing your virginity is *kongkkagi* (콩까기), literally "peeling the bean."

THE BOOBY CONTINUUM))
GAJI GAJI GASEUMDEUL
가지 가지 가슴들

Breastless
Aseupalteue buteun kkumttakji
아스팔트에 붙은 껌딱지
Literally, "flat gum on an asphalt street." You will see these on many
Korean girls, who are stick thin anyways.

Flat-chested
Jeollbyeok
절벽

Barely breasted
Binyakhan gaseum
빈약한 가슴

Medium-breasted
Adamhan gaseum
아담한 가슴

Ample-breasted
Geullaemeo
굴래머

Big tits
Geoyu
거유

Ginormous tits
Jeotso
젖소
Literally, "milking cow."

Beautiful tits
Chakhan gaseum
착한 가슴
Literally, "nice breasts." In Korea, a beautiful appearance makes
you a "nice person." Therefore, if you have beautiful tits, guys will
call you nice and kind. Works out, doesn't it?

Fake boobs
Bbongaseum
뽕가슴

g-spot.
ji spot
지_스팟

> **Where is your g-spot?**
> *Neoji spotsi eohdiya?*
> 너 지|스팟이 어디야?

pussy lips.
eumsun
음순

pubes. (female)
bojiteol
보지털

pussy juice.
aeaek
애액

·····Sexual acts
Seongyo
성교

Sometimes missionary sex just won't cut it. Sometimes you just feel the need go all reverse cowgirl and fingerbang your lover's butthole during a mid-afternoon gangbang. It's perfectly natural. There's no need to be ashamed of your female ejaculation while your boyfriend tittyfucks you in the midst of a Cleveland Steamer. Everybody does it.

> **I am at a perverted age now.**
> *Nado jingeureowun naiya.*
> 나도 **징그러운** 나이야.

> **Have you ever had anal sex?**
> *Hangmun seongyo haebwasseo?*
> 항문 성교 해봤어?

> **I want to do some...**
> *...hago sipeo.*
> ...하고 싶어.

I'm tired of...

... haneungeon jaemiupsseo.

... 하는건 재미없어.

kissing.
Bbobbo
뽀뽀

> **Give me a kiss to remember!**
> *Oneureul ginyeom halmanhan **bbobbo**haejwo!*
> 오늘은 기념 할만한 뽀뽀해줘!

French kissing.
Kiss
키스

foreplay.
Aemu
애무

skinship.
Skinship
스킨쉽

finger banging.
Soneuro
손으로

> **Finger me!**
> *Soneuro haejwo!*
> 손으로 해줘!

cunnilingus.
Yeoseong gugang aemu
여성 구강 애무

> **Go down on me.**
> *Ibeuro haejwo.*
> 입으로 해줘.

fellatio.
Namseong gugang aemu
남성 구강 애무

> **Give me a blow job.**
> *Ibeuro haejwo.*
> 입으로 해줘.

Wanna try…?
…haeboja?
… 해보자?

I like…
Nan … joahae.
난 … 좋아해.

> **swallowing.**
> *samkidanuengirl*
> 삼키는걱

> **cumming on the face.**
> *eolgurae ssaneungirl*
> 얼굴에 싸는걱

> **sixty-nine.**
> *yukgu*
> 육구

> **titty-fucking.**
> *gaseum sex*
> 가슴 섹스

> **missionary style.**
> *apchigi*
> 앞치기

> **doggy-style.**
> *dwichigi*
> 뒤치기

> **woman on top.**
> *maltagi*
> 맏타기
> Literally, "riding horse."

Threesome
Sseurisseom
쓰리썸

Group sex
Group sex
그룹 섹스

Gangbang
Dollimbbang
돌림빵

Anal
Aeneol
애널

> **Do it in my asshole.**
> *Ttonkkumeongeuro haejwo.*
> 똥구멍으로 해줘.

Female ejaculation
Yeoseong sajeong
여성 사정

•••••Orgasm
Oreugajeum
오르가즘

Do it...
...hae.
...해.

> **faster, faster.**
> *Bballi bballi*
> 빨리 빨리
>
> **slower.**
> *Cheoncheonhi*
> 천천히
>
> **harder.**
> *Ssege*
> 세게
>
> **softer.**
> *Salsal*
> 살살
>
> **more.**
> *Deo*
> 더

This hurts.
Apa.
아파.

This feels really good.
Gibun joa.
기분 좋아.

I'm getting a hard-on.
Seosseo.
섰어.

I'm starting to get off.
Neukkimi wa.
느낌이 와.

I want to come.
Ssago sipeo.
싸고 싶어.

I'm about to come.
Ssallyeogo geurae.
쌀려고 그래.

Where do you want it?
Eodiro hallae?
어디로 할래?

I'm coming!
Na ssalkeogata!
나 쌀거같아!

Did you have an orgasm?
Neo neukkyeosseo?
너 느꼈어?
Literally, "Did you feel it?"

I just came all over.
Bangeum ssasseo.
방금 쌌어.

I had a wet dream.
Na mongjeong haesseo.
나 몽정했어.

I need to beat off. (male)
Na ttalttari chyeoyahae.
나 딴딴이 쳐야해.

Go masturbate.
Jawihae.
자위해.

•••••Sexcessories
Sex toy
섹스토이

Do you have a ...?
~isseo?
~있어?

Let's try using a...
~sseoboja.
~ 써보자.

> **condom.**
> *Condom*
> 콘돔
>
>> **Do you have a condom?**
>> *Neo condom gajigo isseo?*
>> 너 콘돔 가지고 있어?
>
> **dildo.**
> *Dildo*
> 딜도
>
>> **Where can I get a dildo?**
>> *Neo dildo eodieseo guhae?*
>> 너 딜도 어디에서 구해?
>
> **vibrator.**
> *Baibeureiteo*
> 바이브레이터

Do you like my fingers or your vibrator better?
*Neo nae songaragi joa anim **baibeureiteo**ro*
haneunge deo joa?
너 내 손가락이 좋아 아닌 **바이브레이터**로
하는게 더 좋아?

Let's watch...
... *boja.*
... 보자.

porn.
Poreuno
포르노

It's illegal to film porn in Korea, but you can import it from abroad. A while ago, some high school students filmed themselves having sex and made a video called *Red Scarf* (*bbalgan mahoora*; 빨간 마후라). The video got leaked and became a big deal in Korea.

adult videos.
Adult video
어덜트 비디오

These films are usually found in Korean love motels. Unfortunately they're pretty tame compared to American porns (you don't even get to see any pussy or cock—lame!).

·····Your sexuality
Neoeui seonghyang
너의 성향

Scholars often talk about the virgin-whore dichotomy of women's sexuality. But what about the butch-fem polarity and the pimp-ho binary? Where do all the call-girls, players, born-again virgins, bisexuals, premature ejaculators, and S&M freaks fit in to the spectrum? Well, in the wide world of Korean slang, there's a place for all you freaky sex fiends. So come on in. It's warm in here.

I love a good slut.
*Naneun **geolle** joahae.*
나는 **걸레** 좋아해.

I'm a...
Naneun …ya.
나는 … 야.

virgin.
cheonyeo
처녀

ancient virgin.
cheonyeonkinyeommul
천연기념물
Known as a "national treasure" or "never been kissed" for both boys and girls.

30-something unmarried woman.
nocheonyeo
노처녀

whore.
changnyeo
창녀

call-girl.
call geol
콜걸

underage prostitute.
wonjogyoje
원조교제

Homosexual
Dongseongaeja
동성애자

Gay
Geyi
게이

Lesbian
lejeubieon
레즈비언

Bisexual
Yangseongaeja
양성애자

Queer
Horosaekki
호로새끼

Pimp
Gidungseobang
기둥서방

Playboy
Baramdungi
바람둥이

Quickdraw
Tokki
토끼
Literally, "rabbit."

Premature ejaculation
Joru
조루

Impotent
Balgibujeon
발기부전

Sadist
Saedist
세디스트

Masochist
Maesokist
메소키스트

Pervert
Byeontae
변태

Two-timer
Yangdari
양다리

Player
Muneodari
문어다리

> **Did you hear? That player got STD for sleeping around.**
> *Waeniriya, jeonom **muneodari** geolchidaga seongbyeong ormatde.*
> 왠일이야, 저놈 **문어다리** 걸치다가 성병 옮았데.

CHAPTER 6

ANGRY KOREAN

HANGUK YOK

한국 욕

Just because Koreans are smaller than your average white dude doesn't mean they get pushed around. They can be some badass motherfuckers. And what they lack in size they make up for with an impressive array of insults, swear words, smack downs and verbal abuse directed toward the size of their enemy's genitals. You've been warned.

Enemies

Jeok

적

I hate my...
Nan nae ...ga sireo.
난 내 ... 가 싫어.

boss.
sangsa
상사

I'm so mad at my asshole boss.
*Geu **sangsa** gaesaekkittaemune yeolbada jukkesseo.*
그 **상사** 개새끼때문에 역받아 죽겠어.

rival.
waensu
왠수

> **I am fucked because of my rival.**
> *Na geu **waensu**ttaemune jot dwaesseo.*
> 나 그 **왠수**때문에 좆 됐어.

My...is a real asshole.
Nae ...neun jinjja sibalnomiya.
내 ... 는 진짜 시발놈이야.

ex-girlfriend
jeon yeochin
전 여친

> **My ex-girlfriend is a slut.**
> *Nae **jeon yeoichin** ssipalnyeon.*
> 내 **전 여친** 씨팔년.

ex-boyfriend
jeon namchin
전 남친

> **My ex-boyfriend is a psycho.**
> *Nae **jeon namchin** michinnom. / ttorai.*
> 내 **전 남친** 미친놈. / 또아이.

teacher (unpopular)
kkondae
꼰대

> **My shitty teacher tried to say that I didn't do my homework.**
> *Nae **kkondae**ga nabogo sookjereul an haetdaneun geoya.*
> 내 **꼰대**가 나보고 숙제를 안 했다는 거야.

mother-in-law
sieomeoni (husband's mom) / jangmonim (wife's mom)
시어머니 / 장모님

My **mother-in-law** has lost her mind.
Sieomeoni nomang nasyeosseo.
시어머니 노망 나셨어.

Politician
Jeongchi-in
정치인

All **politicians** are con-artists.
Jungchi-indeureun da sagikkuniya.
정치인들은 다 사기군이야.

Police
Gyeongchal
경찰

Cops
Jjapsae
짭새

Shit, the **cops** are coming.
*Ssibal **jjapsae** tteotda.*
씨밭 **짭새** 떳다.

•••••Pissed off
Yeolbatda
역받다

Sometimes, shit pisses you off. It's important to know the proper verbiage in order to fully convey this emotion to others around you. Otherwise, you may have to cut a bitch.

Damn!
Bireomeogeul!
빌어먹을!

Shit!
Jenjang!
젠장!

Fuck!
Ssibal!
씨발!

I'm in a bad mood today, so don't get on my nerves!
*Oneul na **gibun ggulggul**hanikka geondeulji ma!*
오늘 나 **기분 꿀꿀**하니까 건드지 마!

Get away from me!
Kkeojeo!
꺼져!

Don't make me angry!
***Yeol batge** hajima!*
역 받게 하지마!

I am going to kill you!
***Jugyeo**beorinda!*
죽어버린다!
This is a very popular phrase
used lightly, and isn't normally
life threatening.

Leave me alone.
Geunyang naebido.
그냥 내비둬.

None of your business!
Gwansimggeo!
관심꺼!

Don't worry about me!
Sangwanma!
상관마!

You're bothering me!
Gwichana!
귀찮아!

You're so annoying!
Jjajeungna!
짜증나!

You're pissing me off with your whining!
Neoga jjingjjingdaeseo jjangna!
너가 찡찡대서 **짱나**!

My head is about to explode!
Ttukkeong yeollinda!
뚜껑 열린다!
Literally, "My pot cover is about to boil open."

·····Smack talk
Yokseol
욕설

Koreans like to talk shit, and the most commonly used insult is "crazy." Whenever you come across someone that pisses you off, calling them crazy under your breath is a great way to warm up your shit talking. Whoever comes up with the most creative smack talk about the other person's appearance/ hygiene/mother's dirty sex life is the winner!

That bitch is crazy!
Jeo nyeon michin nyeoniya!
저년 **미친년**이야!

You're a punk ass.
Meorie pido an mareunge.
머리에 피도 안 마른게.
Literally, "Your head is still blood-wet from your mom's womb."

How is it possible to be so stupid?
Eotteoke geureoke baboilsuga innya?
어떻게 그렇게 **바보**일수가 있냐?

What a moron!
Meogcheogi saekki!
멍청이 새끼!

RACiSTS)))
INJONGCHABYEOLJA
인종차별자

People often assume that South Koreans don't like North Koreans, but the truth is that North Koreans are often the friends and family of their neighbors to the south. The people that Koreans really hate are the Japanese. And who can blame them? Japan colonized Korea for 36 years until the 1940s. That shit tends to breed hostility. Other than the Japanese, who Koreans hate with a special passion, Koreans are ready to insult everybody with pretty much equal opportunity.

Get outta my face you dumb ...
Jeolluu ggeojeo, i meojeori gateun ...
전루 꺼져, 이 머저리같은...

Yankee.
yangki.
양키.

cracker.
hayanbbang.
하얀빵.

nigger.
kkamdungi.
깐둥이.

Jap. (Japanese)
Jjokbari. / Ilbonnom. / Woenom.
쪽발이. / 일본놈. / 왜놈.

Chink. (Chinese)
Jjanggae.
짱개.

Gook. (North Korean)
Bbalgaengi.
빨갱이.

She's such a bitch!
*Jeoreon gae gateun **nyeon**!*
저런 개같은 **년**!

Son of a bitch!
Gaesaekki!
개새끼!

I'm gonna beat that asshole.
Jeo ssibalnom pae jugilggeoya.
저 씨발눔 패 죽일꺼야.

Rude people suck.
Ssagagi upneun nom / nyeon jaesu eopsseo.
싸가지 없는 눔 / 년 재수없어.

Does lusting after Miley Cyrus make me a bad person?
Miley Cyrus joahamyeon na nabbeunnominya?
마일리 싸이러스 좋아하면 나 나쁜눔이냐?

He's nothing but trash.
Jeo saekkineun sseuregi bakke andwae.
저 새끼는 쓰레기 밖에 안돼.

I hate rotten people!
Sseogeul nomdeul neomu sireo!
썩은 눔들 너무 싫어!

She has a bad attitude.
Jeonyeon seongkkal deureoweo.
저년 성깔 드러워.

You're nuts!
Ttoraigateun!
똘아이 같은!

Quit being such a bastard!
Horosaekki gateun jit jom geumanhae!
호로새끼 같은 짓 좀 그만해!

Don't be a crybaby!
Ulbojit hajima!
울보짓 하지마!

> **Santa won't give a gift to a crybaby.**
> *Santaneun Ulbohante sunmul an jundae.*
> 산타는 울보한테 선물 안 준대.
> Korean mothers use this saying when trying to convince their
> whiny little bitch kids to shut up.

Cheapskate
Jjandori / Jjansuni
짠돌이 / 짠순이

> **Your boyfriend is a cheapskate.**
> *Neo namjachinguneun neomu jjandoriya.*
> 너 남자친구는 너무 **짠돌이**야.

> **Pay it, you cheapskate!**
> *Don jom sseo, jjandora!*
> 돈 좀 써, **짠돌**아!

You're so foul-mouthed.
Neon ibe geolle mureosseo.
넌 입에 걸레 물었어.

Literally, "You have a dirty rag in your mouth!"

Don't just stand there like a retard and give me a hand!
Byeongsincheoreom geogi seoitjimalgo dowajo!
병신처럼 거기 서있지말고 도와줘!

Your dad is a pervert.
Neone abba byeontaeya.
너네 아빠 **변태**야.

That bullshitter always makes shit up.
Jeo heopungjaengi mennal geojitmalhae.
저 **허풍쟁이** 맨날 거짓말해.

Japanese girls are low class.
Ilbonnyeondeureun ssangnyeondeuriya.
일본년들은 **쌍년**들이야.

That stalker won't stop texting me.
Jeo stokeoga gyesok munjahae.
저 **스토커**가 계속 문자해.

You're a fucking bad luck.
Neo jinjja jaesu upsseop.
너 진짜 **재수없어**.

Korean dudes are lazy.
Hanguk namjadeul ge-eureumbaengideuriya.
한국 남자애들 게으름뱅이들이야.

Men are pigs.
Namjaneun da dwaejiya.
남자는 다 돼지야.

You're worthless.
Neon sseulmo upneun nomiya.
넌 쓸모 없는 놈이야.

You're a parasite.
Ya i bindaesaekkiya.
야 이 빈대새끼야.

·····Snapping
Nun doragannae
눈 돌아갔내

Believe it or not, more than half of Koreans are blood type B, which means that they are prone to be short-tempered according to a wacky but well-known Korean blood-type personality test. So whenever you see someone's eyes go all crazy and they start barking at you for no reason, you can escalate the situation by inferring that they are blood type B and have no control over their emotions. Koreans love hearing this.

Snapping
Nun doragannae
눈 돌아갔내
Literally, "Your eyes have gone crazy."

Careful, dude's about to snap.
Josimhae, je nun doragaryeogohae.
조심해, 제 눈 돌아가려고해.

He's got a real short temper.
Je jinjja dahyeoljiliya.
제 진짜 다혈질이야.

Uh-oh, she's starting to get stand-offish.
Jeobwa, jyae bbeoljjumhaejinja.
저봐, 쟤 **뻘쭘해**진다.

He's giving you the glare.
Jyaega neo noryeobwa.
쟤가 너 **노려봐**.

Are you giving me a dirty look?
Neo na jjaeryeobonya?
너 나 **째려보나**?

Are you insane?
Neo dorannya?
너 **돌았나**?

You're fucking hella crazy! (dramatizing)
Neo jonna dorasseo!
너 **존나 돌았어**!

Lower your eyes!
Nun kkara i gaesaekkiya!
눈깔아 이 개새끼야!
It's considered extremely disrespectful to look at elders straight in their eyes while they are lecturing you.

I'm about to explode.
Na teojigi ilbojikjeoniya.
나 **터지기** 일보 직전이야.

My life is fucked.
Nae paljjaga gaepaljjaya.
내 **팔자**가 개상팔자야.

•••••Fighting words
Ssaulttae sseuneun maldeul
싸울때 쓰는 말들

Guns are illegal in Korea. They're for the military only. So how do Korean cops protect themselves and fight the bad guys?

Why, with whistles and sticks, of course! This may sound wussy to you, but I wouldn't fuck with a Korean cop. Those sticks can pack a mean hit. But if you do fight a cop, or anyone else for that matter, here are some good terms to really push the situation to full-scale violence.

I don't like you.
Neo sireo.
너 싫어.

I hate you.
Neo miwo.
너 미워.

You suck!
Neo wang jesu!
너 왕 제수!

Go away!
Jeoriga!
저리가!

Go to hell.
Jiokga!
지옥가!

Fuck off!
Ggeojyeo!
꺼져!

Fuck you.
Yeotmugeo. / Bbeokyu.
엿먹어. / 뻑큐.

Shut your mouth.
Agari dakchyeo.
아가리 닥쳐.

Shut the fuck up.
Dakchyeo.
닥쳐.

Die!
Jugeullae!
죽을래!
This isn't a real life threat; it's used more commonly as playful smack talk.

What the fuck?
Ssibal igeo moya?
시발 이거 뭐야?

What did you just say?
Dasi malhaebwa?
다시 말해봐?

Let's take it outside.
Bakkeuro nawa.
밖으로 나와.

Bring it on!
Wa! / Haebwa.
와! / 해봐.

You got a problem?
Bulman isseo?
불만 있어?

You picking a fight with me for no reason?
I saram hwangdanghage saramjapne?
이 사람 황당하게 사람잡네?

I'm gonna fuck you up.
Neojugeuljul ara.
너 죽을줄 알아.

I'm gonna kick your ass.
Neo jonna majeuljul ara.
너 존나 맞을줄알아.

I'm gonna beat the shit out of you.
Neo gae paedeusi majeuljul ara.
너 개 패듯이 맞을줄 알아.

Literally, "I am going to beat you up like a dog." It originates from the Korean practice of eating dog meat. To prepare the delicacy, the live canine is beaten with a bat to tenderize the meat. I know, I know, it's morbid, especially if you're PETA vegetarian.

Kneel or die, bitch!
Gaenyeon, an kkureumyeon jukneunda!
개년, 안 꿇으면 죽는다!

I fucked him up!
Jeo saekki yut mugyeosseo!
저 새끼 엿먹였어!

●●●●●Stopping a fight
Ssaum jungjisikigi
싸움 중지시키기

So you're at a bar getting tipsy and talkin' shit about some dude's slutty sister. Next thing you know, dude's got ten friends and all of your crew has dipped out on you like a bunch of pussies. Time to make nice and kiss some proverbial ass.

Hey, let's…
Ya, uri…
야, 그만 …

> **relax.**
> *jinjeonghae.*
> 진정해.

> **compromise.**
> *hwahaehae.*
> 화해해.

> **calm down.**
> *hwanaeji ma.*
> 화내지 마.

I'm sorry.
Mianhae.
미안해.

I apologize.
Sagwa halgge.
사과할게.

It's my fault.
Naega jalmot haesseo.
내가 잘못 했어.

You should understand me!
Neoga ihaehae!
너가 이해해!

Forgive me.
Yongseohaejo.
용서해줘.

Give me one more chance.
Hanbeonman bwajwo.
한번만 봐줘.

Forget about it.
Ijeo beoryeo.
잊어 버려.

It has nothing to do with me.
Narang sangwan eopneun iriya.
나랑 상관 없는 일이야.

Stop it.
Geumanhae.
그만해.

Don't do it.
Hajima.
하지마.

It's already in the past.
Da jinan iriya.
다 지난 일이야.

Whatever.
Dwaesseo.
됐어.

Don't go.
Gagima!
가지마!

I'm going to call the cops.
Jjapsae bureunda.
짭새 부른다.

Call 112!
Singohanda!
신고한다!

"112" is the emergency number to call the cops in Korea.

CHAPTER 7

POPPY KOREAN

HANGUK YUHAENGEO

한국 유행어

As with many Asian countries, American pop culture has had a huge influence in Korea. Fast food chains like McDonald's are ubiquitous, and Western-style fashion is all the rage. But Korean culture is made up of more than just Western rip-offs. In the past few years there has been a surge in exports of Korean pop culture, including TV dramas, music and movies. Dubbed the "Korean Wave," the cultural phenomenon helped raise Korea's profile and boost tourism.

·····TV

TV

티비

There are four main Korean TV channels: SBS, KBS1, KBS2 and MBC. These stations show the most popular shows on TV. Korean TV shows don't have many commercial breaks—unlike those on American TV. (Seriously, did you ever watch

The Chappelle Show? There were more commercial breaks than jokes on that show. I'm still mad about this. Come back to us, Dave. Come back!)

Let's watch a...
...*boja.*
... 보자.

soap opera.
Drama
드라마

Well-known for love triangles and tragic storylines, Korean dramas (akin to American soap operas) are extremely popular throughout Asia. Korean television shows have gotten so popular that tons of Japanese tourists come to Korea to visit the areas where the scenes were filmed. Popular dramas include *Winter Sonata*, *Iris*, *Queen Seokdeok*, *Boys Over Flower* and *Jewel in the Palace*.

Queen Seondeok is a badass **TV show**!
*Seondeok yeowangeun eomcheongnan **drama**ya.*
선덕여왕은 엄청난 **드라마**야.

comedy.
Gaegeu
개그

KOREAN TV SHOWS

High Kick!
Jibungttulko Haikick
지붕뚫고 하이킥

Literally, "High kick through the roof." This immensely popular sitcom portrays three generations of family members living together under one roof and getting into hijinks. Ever seen *Everybody Loves Raymond*? Kinda like that but everyone stuffed into the same house.

Ya, i bbangkku ttongkkuya!
야 이 빵꾸똥꼬야!

Literally, "fart and anal." This catch phrase from *High Kick!* has made its way into the Korean lexicon. You are basically calling someone stupid in a light-hearted, adorable way.

Uchassa / Gaegeuconsseoteu
웃찾사 / 개그콘서트

Korean comedy uses a lot of self-deprecating humor and can be really hilarious. These two programs should provide some yucks—they're like *Saturday Night Live* with some stand-up thrown in. Koreans have no problem creating comedy gold by talking shit about themselves.

Infinite Challenge
Muhandojeon
무한도전

Infinite Challenge is similar in concept to *Amazing Race* and *American Idol*. The difference is that the contestants are popular celebrities like Jae-suk Yoo (유재석), Hyeong-don Jeong (정형돈), Myung-soo Park (박명수), Hong-chul No (노홍철), Jun-ha Jun (정준하) and Gil (길)—all middle-aged, goofy entertainers. This show has become so popular that it has guest celebrities from all over the world like Paris Hilton, Tiger Woods, Maria Sharapova and soccer star Thierry Daniel Henry.

Ha, it's a piece of cake!
Cham swibjo-ing!
참 쉽조잉!

This biting catch phrase became popular when *Infinite Challenge* contestant Jae-suk Yoo sarcastically said, "Ha, it's a piece of cake!" to other contestants who were struggling with their missions.

Family Outing
Familiga Tteotda
페밀리가 떳다

In the first season of this reality/variety show, pop stars like Jae-suk Yoo (big time MC), Lee Hyo-ri (the Britney Spears of Korea), Jong-shin Yoon (singer-songwriter) and Jong-guk Kim (popular singer) assume the duties of an everyday Korean family at a different traditional countryside home every week. While the celebrities do the housework, the hard-working family takes a well-deserved vacation.

One Night Two Days
Ilbak I-il
일박이일

Similar to the *The Simple Life*, this show features celebrities visiting the countryside to perform tasks outside their comfort zone. Unlike bitchy socialite stars Paris Hilton and Nicole Richie, however, the Korean counterparts are modest, hard-working celebs—much more appealing to the Korean viewers.

We Got Married
Uri Gyeolhonhaesseoyo
우리 결혼했어요
This surreal reality TV show depicts celebrity couples living pretend married lives. It sounds absurd, but it shows the dynamics of how different people live and work together to make their relationship successful.

Kiss Kiss Kiss
Bbobbobbo
뽀뽀뽀
This is kinda like a Korean *Sesame Street*: A bunch of kids and characters play and dance around and learn valuable life lessons.

·····Movies
Hanguk yeonghwa
한국영화

Korean movies have gained popularity throughout Asia and the U.S. Hollywood has even adapted several Korean movies into American films (e.g., *The Lake House,* starring Keanu Reeves and Sandra Bullock). Of course, I definitely recommend watching the originals. Even with subtitles, you'll get the morals behind the stories rather than just seeing the American glitz and big-name actors.

Old Boy
Old Boy
올드보이
Influenced by Chinese kung fu flicks, this movie broke out of the stereotypical Korean movie storyline, which usually features a love triangle with the inevitable tragic ending. In fact, the style resembles *Kill Bill*, which also borrows heavily from China's distinctive action movies. From the movie:

Who are you?
Nugunya neon?
누구냐 넌?

Sympathy for Lady Vengeance

Chinjeolhan Geumjassi

친절한 금자씨

Cut from the same cloth as *Old Boy* (it is done by the same director, Chan-wook Park), this movie stars Young-ae Lee, one of Korea's top ingénue actresses who is known for her innocent roles. Here, she's opened up a can of bad ass and transformed herself into a revenge-seeking murderer. From the movie:

Do good to yourself.
Neona jal hasaeyo.
너나 잘 하세요.

My Sassy Girl

Yeopgijeogin Geunyeo

엽기적인 그녀

If you want to get a Korean girlfriend, watch this movie and learn how to become her servant. If you're in Korea looking for a submissive Asian girl, you're knocking on the wrong door — try Japan. From the movie:

Do you wanna die?
Jugeullae?
죽을래?

The Lake House

Siworae

시월에

Sandra Bullock and Keanu Reeves ruined this movie in the American version. *Damn*, the Hollywood remake's time-travel sequences don't make any sense at all!

A Tale of Two Sisters

Janghwa Hongryeon

장화 홍련

Cinderella's and Snow White's evil stepmothers pale in comparison to the Korean stepmom in *A Tale of Two Sisters*. This horror flick is based on the Korean traditional tale *Janghwa*

CARTOONS)))
MANHWA
만화

Anime
Ilbon manhwa yeonghwa
일본만화영화

Japanese anime is very popular in Korea. *Sailor Moon*, *Pokemon*, *Dragonball* and other classics were airing here way before they were imported to America. If you're an anime fan you'll find a lot of friends in Korea. Let your geek flag fly!

Animation (usually refers to Korean anime)
Manhwa yeonghwa
만화영화

Protagonists in Korean animations are more human than the fantastical, sci-fi characters with magical powers coming out of Japan. Some of the most famous shows are Dooyi (둘리)—the story of a time-traveling baby dinosaur; Hani (하니)—the tale of an orphan girl who becomes a runner; and Dokgotak (독고탁)—the story of a poor young boy who becomes a famous baseball player.

Manga
Manhwachaek
만화책

Being a comic-book nerd may not get you laid in the U.S., but you don't need to be shy about reading *manhwachaek* in Korea. It's an accepted part of pop culture and people talk about comic book characters like they're family members. A lot of *manhwachaek* stories get reproduced as TV shows and movies.

Hongryeon. Hollywood did a lame version (*The Uninvited*) and failed miserably! Viva Korean movies!

Swiri
쉬리

A spy story of North and South Korea. The lead actress, Yun-jin Kim, is probably best known in the U.S. for her role in the TV series *Lost*.

Mother
Mother
마더

Mothers will do anything for their children, but the mom in this pic really goes to the extreme. When the lead character's retarded but sweet (in her eyes) son is arrested for murder, she decides to independently find the "real" murderer. It's a very uncomfortable psychological thriller with lots of close-up shots chronicling the emotional intensity. You will like it (cuz I tell you to).

Below are popular Korean movies that have been bought/co-produced by Hollywood and opened (and closed quickly) in the U.S.:

Thirst
Bakjwi
박쥐
A Christian priest undergoes surgery to become a vampire.

Host
Gwoemul
괴물
A mutated monster attacks Seoul; known as being the first Korean CGI movie entirely produced and animated within the country.

D-War
Diwo
디워
A former comedian, the dinosaur-obsessed Hyung-rae Shim came to Hollywood and made this film, which took seven years. *D-War* deals with Korean mythology of a special 1,000-year-old snake that would eventually become a dragon and rule the world.

·····Music
Eumak
음악

Let's listen to some…
…*deutja.*
…듣자.

Let's bump some...
...teulja.
... 틀자.

I wanna hear some...
Na ... deutgo sipeo.
나 ... 듣고 싶어.

K-pop.
pop
팝

Korean Pop. The biggest K-pop singer is Rain, Korea's answer to Justin Timberlake. He has toured Asia and been in several Hollywood movies. But if you ask me, most of his music sounds are unlistenable, re-hashed '80s pop garbage.

ballad.
ballad
발라드

Seung-hoon Shin (신승훈) is the Korean king of ballads. (Side note: For some reason, there aren't many female balladeers in Korea.) Most ballads are popularized when they become the theme songs to TV shows.

rock.

rock

락

Rock is a somewhat strange genre to Koreans; they believe rock singers are dark, weird people. But rockers need not despair: Do-hyun Yoon and a group called Boohwal (부활), meaning "rebirth," fill this small niche.

indie.

indie

인디

You can find a lot of Indie rock musicians in the Hongdae district.

rap.

rap

랩

My favorite rap group is Drunken Tiger. Their lyrics are genius.

reggae.

reggae

레게

Gun-mo Kim (김건모) is a self-proclaimed reggae artist. He's not great, but he's the best we got.

pop group.

pop group

팝 구릅

When 'N Sync and Destiny's Child were storming the pop charts in the '90s, the boy/girl-band trend caught on in Korea. Since then, there have been several successful groups such as HOT, Super Jr., Sechs Kies, Big Bang, SES and Finkl. Current girl groups Brown Eyed Girls, Wonder Girls (who even toured with the Jonas Brothers) and Girls' Generation have gotten so popular that Chinese imitations have sprung up.

Do you know how to dance Wonder Girls' "Tell me" dance?

Neo Wonder Girls tellmechum chuljjurareo?

너 원더걸스 텔미춤 출줄알아?

If you don't know this dance move, you're considered a stranger. Watch it on YouTube to learn it.

·····Computer / Internet
Computer / Internet
컴퓨터 / 인터넷

Korea is at the forefront for adopting and implementing new technology. Even the high-speed Internet that you see in the U.S. is too slow for them—Korea's upgraded their entire infrastructure to the ultra-ultra-fast fiber-optic connection that's not available to all Americans. And to further put Americans to shame, Koreans are rumored to be the best hackers around.

Cyworld
Cyworld
싸이월드
Facebook and MySpace may be big in the U.S., but in Korea it's all about Cyworld—everybody's on it.

Do you have a Cyworld account?
Neo cyhae?
너 싸이해?

Online videos
Dongyeongsang
동영상

Pandora TV
Pandora TV
판도라 티비
Pandora TV is YouTube-plus. It's basically cable shows on the Internet, kind of like podcasts on iTunes.

Hit me up on AIM.
Nate on eseo bwa.
네이트온에서 봐.

Wanna have a video chat session tonight?
Oneul bame hwasangchatting halkka?
오늘 밤에 화상채팅할까?

naver.com / daum.net
naver / daum
네이버 / 다음
These sites are the Google and Yahoo search engine equivalents.

Who needs books when you have search engines?
Geomsaek enjini itneunde chaegi wae piryohae?
검색엔진이 있는데 책이 왜 필요해?

iNSTANT MESSAGING)))
CHATTING HALTTAE HANEUNMAL
체팅할때 하는말

@
golbaengi
골뱅이

emoticon
emoticon
이모티콘

OTL / OZL
오티엘 / 오지엘
This emoticon is used when you're feeling down and self-deprecating. It's a full-body profile of a human figure down on its hands and knees. O is the head, T is the upper torso and hands and L is the shape of legs. With OZL, the "Z" indicates the figure down on the forearms instead.

hehe
ㅎㅎ

keke
ㅋㅋ

=)
^.^

=0
^e^

Y-Y
ㅜ.ㅜ / ㅠ.ㅠ

duo.co.kr
duo
듀오
This is the biggest online Korean dating site—like Match.com but not as sleazy.

We met on a dating site.
*Uri **date ssaiteu** eseo mannasseo.*
우리 **데이트 싸이트**에서 만났어.

My computer is down.
*Nae **computer** downdwaesseo.*
내 **컨퓨터** 다운됐어.

I've never used a Mac before.
*Na **mac** hanbeondo sseobonjeok upsseo.*
나 **맥** 한번도 써본적 없어.
Macs aren't popular in Korea.

I saw an iPod yesterday and it was beautiful.
*Eojae **iPod** bwatneunde ibbeudeora.*
어제 **아이팟** 봤는데 이쁘더라.

•••••Cell phone
Handphone
핸드폰

Korea leads the world in cell phone technology. Companies are constantly updating the models and it's considered a status symbol to have the most up-to-date phone.

iPhone
A-I-pon
아이폰

Samsung Omnia phone
Omnia
옴니아

LG Prada phone
Pradapon
프라다폰

Video phone chat
Hwasangtonghwa
화상통화

Text message
Munjja
문자

Digital Mobil Broadcast
DMB
디엠비
All Koreans can watch TV from their cells if they subscribe to
DMB. The signal is strong enough to even work underground.
This comes in handy in Korea since so many people use the
subterranean public transit system.

·····Fashion
Fashion
패션

Korean fashion trends are lifted directly from America pop
culture and Korean TV shows. Whatever popular actors and
actresses are wearing instantly becomes trendy.

Sell-out celebrity
Wanpannyeo / nam
완판녀 / 남
Celebrities who cash in on their fame by shamelessly wearing their
endorsement products. And it works—the stuff sells out at stores!

Check out the **trendy hair** on that K-pop dude!
*Jeo hanguk yeonaein **yuhaenghan meori** style bwa!*
저 한국 연애인 **유행한 머리** 스타일 봐!
In 2009, the wavy hairstyle (*mulkyul meori* style; 물결머리) was
popular for women and the turban shell hairstyle (*sora meori* style;
소라머리) was big for men.

I love your retro look.
*Neo **bokgopung** gwaenchanta.*
너 **복고풍** 괜찮다.

White-washed jeans are so vintage.
*Mul bbajin cheongbajineun **bintiji** lookiya.*
물 빠진 청바지는 **빈티지** 룩이야.

I love Lil Weezy's hip-hop swag.
*Nan Lil Weezy **hip-hop** style-i joteora.*
난 리를 위지 **힙합** 스타일이 좋더라.

The power tie really makes the business style.
*Nektaireul maeya **jeongjang style**-iya.*
넥타이를 매야 **정장 스타일**이야.
You can forget about casual Fridays in Korea—all businessmen wear suits. Period.

Korean chicks are always so trendy.
*Hanguk yeojadeureun eonjena **trendy**hae.*
한국 여자들은 언제나 **트랜디**해.

The mainstream look is soooo boring.
*Yuhaenghan **look**eun neomu jigyeowo.*
유행한 룩은 너무 지겨워.

Your mom has awesome style.
*Neone eommaneun **sikhae**.*
너네 엄마는 **시크해**.

Lookin' stylish!
***Meotjaengine**!*
멋쟁이네!

Damn, Lady Gaga is looking tacky!
*Lady Gaga **chontinanda**.*
레이디 가가 **촌티난다**.

·····Horror
Gongpo
공포

Koreans love horror stories—they're especially popular in the summer when Koreans watch tons of scary TV shows and movies (in air-conditioned comfort) to forget about the sweltering weather.

Scary story
Museowun yaegi
무서운 얘기

Tell me a ghost story.
***Gwisinyaegi** haejwo.*
귀신얘기 해줘.

It's scary.
Museopda.
무섭다.

Scary school stories
Hakgyo gwoedam
학교 괴담
Korean people love scary stories about students that die in school. It's one of the more animated topics of conversation that students discuss when hanging out after school.

Ghost
Gwisin
귀신

Virgin ghost
Cheonyeo gwisin
처녀귀신

Most Korean scary stories have ghosts, but odds are the ghost is a virgin who meets an unfortunate death before marriage. This keeps her coming back to the real world to avenge her wrongful death. Another popular ghost character is called *dalgyal gwisin* (달걀귀신), meaning "egg ghost" because of its lack of face.

Exorcist
Twoemasa
퇴마사

Chinese zombie
Gangssi
강시

The Chinese Zombie is prevalent in Korean movies and comics. Normally they can be defeated by a *bujeok* (부적), or paper charm. If only all threats were that simple.

Fortune teller
Jeomjaengi
점쟁이

Korean fortune tellers don't use crystal balls to see your future. They ask for names and birthdays to tell your fortune.

> ### Tell me my **fortune.**
> ***Jeom*** *bwajuseyo.*
> 점 봐주세요.

Shaman
Mudang
무당

The Korean shaman is typically summoned to comfort ghosts.

Korean monster
Dokkaebi
도깨비

Similar to the Japanese *oni*, the *dokkaebi* is a gargoyle-looking character that has its own magic bat called *dokkaebi bangmangi* (도깨비 방망이). It's known for its mischievous behavior to scare bad people.

Death god
Jeoseungsaja
저승사자
This character wears a black outfit with a traditional Korean hat (*gat*; 갓) made of horsetail. He comes to drag you to the underworld.

CHAPTER 8

SPORTY KOREAN
HANGUK SPORTS YONGEO
한국 스포츠 용어

Koreans are some of the most competitive people in the world, so they don't mess around when it comes to sports. Soccer is big and anybody who watches the Olympics will know that Koreans kick some serious ass in speed skating. For real, they clean up golds in this sport like nobody's business.

•••••Sports
Sports / Undong
스포츠 / 운동

Do you like sports?
*Neo **undong** joahae?*
너 **운동** 좋아해?

What sport do you play?
*Neo eotteon **undong** jalhae?*
너 어떤 **운동** 잘해?

What's your team?
*Neo nugu **pyeon**iya?*
너 누구 **편**이야?

Who's team are you on?
*Neo nae **pyeon**iya je pyeoniya?*
너 내 **편**이야 제 편이야?

Who's your favorite player?
*Niga jel joahaneun **sunsu**ga nuguya?*
니가 젤 좋아하는 **선수**가 누구야?

Let's watch…
Uri … boja.
우리 … 보자.

Let's play…
Uri … haja.
우리 … 하자.

> **basketball.**
> *nongu*
> 농구
>
> **baseball.**
> *yagu*
> 야
>
>> **Strike**
>> *Heot swing*
>> 헛 스윙
>>
>> **Home run**
>> *Home run*
>> 혼런
>
> **volleyball.**
> *baegu*
> 배구
>
> **golf.**
> *golf*
> 골프

Let's go...
Uri ... hareo gaja.
우리 ... 하러 가자.

running.
dalligi
달리기

> **I have a cramp in my leg!**
> *Darie jwinasseo!*
> 다리에 쥐났어!
>
> **Do you want to go for a run?**
> *Uri ttwilkka?*
> 우리 뛸까?
>
> **I'm out of breath!**
> *Na sumcha!*
> 나 숨차!

swimming.
suyeong
수영

> **swimming pool**
> *suyeongjang*
> 수영장
>
> **Tae-hwan Park really tears it up in the pool!**
> *Park Tae-hwan jinjja mulkkaeya!*
> 박태환 진짜 물개야!
> Literally, "Tae-hwan Park is a seal!"

Billiards
Dangu
당구

> **Let's go for a game of billiards.**
> *Dangu hanpan hareo gaja.*
> 당구 한판 하러 가자.

Inline skating
Inline skate
인라인 스케이트

Bicycling
Jajeongeo tagi
자전거 타기

Taekwondo
Taekwondo
태권도

This martial art is the national sport of South Korea. *Taekwondo* is loosely translated as "the way of the foot and fist" or "the way of kicking and punching." The basics are taught beginning in elementary school. So don't fuck with a Korean unless you wanna get your face broke.

Soccer
Chukgu
축구

Believe it or not, Korea is pretty bad ass at soccer. In the 2002 World Cup, not only did they host the event, but they ranked fourth. The event brought the whole Korean community together and everyone dressed in red to cheer for the team. It was common during the Cup to sneak your own alcohol into the games and yell at the refs and opposing players. But Korean fans are pretty polite, in general.

> **Shoot!**
> *Shoot!*
> 슛!

Pass the ball!
Pass jom hae!
패스 좀 해!

Gooooooooooal!
Goal~in!
골인!

Rec soccer team
Jogi chukguhoe
조기축구회

Some athletically inclined Korean men wake up before the crack of dawn to play soccer with other crazies, I mean other athletically inclined guys, before they all trudge off to work.

·····Just dance
Chumchwo
춤춰

Dancing is really big in Korea, and TV stations feature a lot of popular dance shows. So you best bring your A-game if you're gonna hit the floor.

Let's **dance**.
Uri chumchuja.
우리 춤추자.

You can't **dance for shit**!
Ireon momchi!
이런 몸치!

Hey, don't **freestyle**, you look like an idiot!
Ya, makchum chujima, eolgani gatah
야, 막춤 추지마, 얼간이 같아!

I love...
Na ... joahae.
나 ... 좋아해.

ballet.
muyong
무용

B-boys.
B-boys
비보이즈

Break dancing wasn't popular in Korea until recently, but
now it's huge and Korean B-boys are some of the best in the
world. The international B-boy competitions are even held in
Seoul.

There are many traditional Korean dances (*hanguk jeontong muyong*; 한국 전통 무용) that you may see while visiting.

Fan dance
Buchaechum
부채춤

During Korean festivals, female dance teams create beautiful
flowers using their bodies and large feathered fans.

Mask dance
Talchum
탈춤

The mask dance is an example of the earliest Korean storytelling
done through dance. This folk art is a theatrical production that
traditionally features male performers—even for female roles.
Check out the Korean film *King and the Clown* (2005)—you'd be
surprised how cute the guys can be in drag.

Sword dance
Kalchum
칼춤

Shamans perform this to summon spirits.

·····Cheering
Eungwon
응원

Cheerleaders in Korea are a bit different from the American
concept. Most strikingly, many of them are males and they
use drums and flags to get the crowd pumped up instead of
booty shorts and fake tits. The most famous cheer team was

the Red Devils from the 2002 World Cup. Korean fans amazed the world with their passion and also for their orderliness after the games. Yup, that's right. Koreans can be orderly!

K-O-R-E-A
Dae-han-min-guk
대한민국

Keep fighting!
Hwaiting!
화이팅!

You're playing great!
Jalhanda!
잘한다!

It's okay!
Gwaenchana!
괜찮아!

Go team!
Uritim jalhanda!
우리팀 잘한다!

We are the champions!
Uriga championiya!
우리가 챔피온이야!

The referee got paid off!
Simpansaekki doneuro maesu dwaesseo!
심판새끼 돈으로 매수됐어!

Booing
Yayu bonaeda
야유 보내다

Boo!
Woo!
우!

This team blows!
I tim byeongsingata!
이 틴 병신같아!

We suck!
Uri jolla mothae!
우리 졸라 못해!

·····Winter sports
Gyeoul sports
겨울 스포츠

The weather gets pretty cold during the winter in Korea. Schools get about a month off for winter break and it's the best time to enjoy winter sports like snowboarding, skiing, skating and sledding. The best places in Korea for winter activities are Muju (무주) and Gangwondo (강원도).

Let's ...
...tareo gaja.
... 타러 가자.

> **snowboard.**
> *Snowboard*
> 스노우보드

> **ski.**
> *Ski*
> 스키

> **ice skate.**
> *Ice skate*
> 스케이트

> **speed skate.**
> *Spid skate*
> 스피드 스케이트
>
> Korean speed skate teams have been one of the top competitors for this category in Olympics. Even U.S team has hired formal medalist Jae-su Chun as their head coach to enhance the performance.

'88 SEOUL OLYMPICS)))
PALPAL SEOUL OLYMPIC
팔팔 서울 올림픽

The 1988 Summer Olympics were held in Seoul, South Korea. North Korea boycotted the event because it's still officially at war with South Korea. But the Games brought a lot of attention to South Korea and really promoted the country's image. It remains an important event in Korean history.

> Hodori
> *hodori*
> 호돌이
> Hodori was the beloved, friendly tiger mascot of the Seoul Olympics.

figure skate.
Figure skate
피겨 스케이트

Korea has been known mainly for its speed skaters, but lately the country has gained recognition in the figure skating arena. Even before winning the 2010 Olympic gold medal, Yu-na Kim was making waves in international competitions. So now the whole world knows—Korea's number one!

sled.
Sseolmae
썰매

·····Fitness
Sinche dallyeon
신체 단련

Korean Standard National Exercise
Gukminchejo
국민체조

Developed by the South Korean government in the 1970s, gookminchejo is a 12-step series of stretches that every kid does, starting in elementary school. And in order to keep the school day free for learning, these organized exercises are held before classes start. How thoughtful.

I'm too fat to do the long jump.
Nan jejari meollittwigi hagien neomu ttungttunghae.
난 제자리 멀리뛰기 하기엔 너무 뚱뚱해.

I can do 1,000...
Na ... 1,000 gae halsuisseo.
나 ... 1,000 개 할수있어.

pull-ups. (men)
teokgeori
턱걸이

In Korea, girls don't really do pull-ups, at least not in the school fitness tests. The gender-specific exercise girls do is called *orae maedalligi* (오래 매달리기), which literally means "dangling." Girls hold the pull-up "up" position (chin above the bar) for as long as their skinny little arms can take it.

sit-ups.
witmom ireukigi
윗몸 일으키기

push-ups.
pal gupyeopigi
팔 굽혀펴기

Benching will get you huge pecs.
Benchinghamyeon geunyuk eomcheongnajyeo.
벤칭하면 근육 엄청나져.

You gotta do squats to hit the glutes.
Dari gupigireul haeya eongdeongiga olaga.
다리굽히기를 해야 엉덩이가 올라가.

My abs are killing me!
Bae ttaengyeo jukkesseo!
배 땡겨 죽겠어!

I'm getting ripped!
Na wanjeon ttanttanhaji!
나 완전 딴딴하지!

You're looking toned.
Mom jom joaboyeo.
몸 좀 좋아보여.

My whole body is sore.
Na on mom ssusyeo.
나 온 몸 쑤셔.

•••••Children's games
Aideul nori
아이들 놀이

Before the invention of addictive sedentary video games, there were simpler juvenile past times that kids enjoyed outside with their friends. With four beautiful and distinct seasons, Korea has always been a huge playground for kids. Some Korean children's games include more physical activity than I would be able to actually do, now that I'm too old and out of shape.

Top
Paengichigi
팽이치기

Kite
Yeonnalligi
연날리기

Hacky sack
Jegichagi
제기 차기

Patty cake
Ssessesse
쎄쎄쎄

Hopscotch
Ttangttameokgi
땅따먹기

MINI OLYMPICS OF KOREA)))
UNDONGHOE
운동회

These mini Olympics are conducted in elementary school and junior high. The whole school gets together and entire families come out to cheer for their kids. It's a lesson in sportsmanship because in Korea, even when you're having fun, you're learning something. For children in Korea, the mini Olympics are as important as the high school prom.

Dodge ball
Pigu
피구
Dodge ball is one of the most popular games in mini Olympics.

Here comes my fireball!
Ja-a, bulkkotshut badara!
자아, 불꽃슛 받아라!

Tug of war
Juldarigi
줄다리기

Sounds you make when you pull the rope!:

Eucha, eucha!
으차, 으차!

Yeongcha, yeongcha!
영차, 영차!

Relay
Relay / ieodalligi
리레이 / 이어달리기

Korean piñata
Bakteoteurigi
박터트리기
Instead of hitting it with a bat, there are two separate piñatas for each team. Whoever throws many bean bags to pop open the pinata wins this game.

Gonggi
Gongi
공기
Gonggi is a similar to Jacks. It's played using five colorful plastic tokens called gongitdol. Each player tosses the tokens on the

ground and throws one into the air. They have to scoop up the others and then proceed to catch the airborne one. There are five levels, and players score points by tossing all five gongitdol and then catching them on the back of their hand. Play proceeds until the airborne token is dropped or other tokens are touched or moved unintentionally. It's sort of gay to play this if you are a full-grown man, but the game can be very entertaining.

Horseback game
Malttukbakki
맡뚝박기
Sadly, this game doesn't involve an actual horse. It's a rough game mainly played by boys. Two teams are chosen and one team becomes the horse post. The "horses" make a chain by bending over and sticking their heads between their teammates' legs. The competing team then hops on the back of other team without letting it fall apart. When all the teammates are on the competitors back, the team leader plays Rock Paper Scissors with the other team leader to decide who will be the winner. It's popular with everyone from children to university students.

·····Traditional Korean games
Minsoknori
민속놀이

Yut board game
Yutnori
윷놀이
Yut is a board game about raising livestock that's usually played during the Korean New Year.

Korean wrestling
Ssireum
씨름
Of course there has to be a game where guys all get worked up and show their strength. Like sumo wrestling, fat men in diapers rub against each other to knock the other guy down or out of the ring. The winner used to get a bull for the prize, so it was a big deal a long time ago. Now, not so much—it's a dying sport cuz most of the athletes have moved on to Ultimate Fighting.

The Korean Wrestling Champion of the Year (the strongest man)

Cheonhajangsa

천하장사

Mock cavalry battle

Gimajeon

기마전

Like the game you play in the pool, only on a mass scale. A group is divided into two teams to play a mock cavalry battle in which the "knights" ride on the shoulders of the "horses" who carry them to battle.

Korean cockfight

Dakssaum

닭싸움

It's not what you think, assuming you were thinking about chickens fighting each other to the death. (If you weren't, you have a dirty, dirty mind and may be addicted to porn.) In the Korean cockfight, two people stand on one leg and support their other leg with their hands. They hop toward each other and try to make their competitor let go of their leg first.

Korean chess
Jangi
장기

Jangi, derived from Chinese Xiangqi, is a strategic board game popular in Korea. The playing board is 9 lines wide by 10 lines long.

Checkmate!
Jangiyo!
장이요!

Go
Baduk
바둑

Featured in the movie *A Beautiful Mind*, Go is a board game noted for its strategic complexity despite its simple rules. The world's Go champions have always been Koreans, not Japanese or Chinese. Perhaps it's time for the international name to be changed to Baduk.

·····Video games
Video game
비디오 게임

Have I mentioned that Korean kids (mostly boys) love to play video games? Guys can sit in front of their computers killing all those little monsters for days without much rest. The addiction is so extreme, it's even killed someone. No, not like the violent American who shot his mom in the head when she took away his Xbox. A Korean teenager was found dead after locking himself in a room for a week. He played video games alone, without sleeping or eating, and his body eventually just stopped working from lack of nutrients and pure exhaustion. Other than that incident, I think video games are actually good for stimulating your brain. Try to battle your way into the world of Korean gamers.

I can't wait to play the new…
Saero naon … jeongmal hagosipeo.
새로 나온 … 정말 하고싶어.

Lineage and special force.
leenigi
리니지

In this popular online game, players can work their way to the pro leagues. They can become professional gamers and make up to $100,000 per year sponsored by big corporations like LG and Samsung.

World of Warcraft (WoW).
WoW game
와우 게임

Starcraft.
Starcraft
스타크레프트

The enemy is at 3 o'clock!
Jeogi saesi banghyange itda!
적이 3시 방향에 있다!

He's using the cheat key!
Chiteuki sseunda!
치트키 쓴다!

He's using Mat hack!
Mathaek sseunda!
맵핵 쓴다!

·····Gambling
Dobak
도박

Seoul's got a gambling area, but Koreans aren't allowed in. Casinos are only for visiting foreigners. So if you wanna be a high roller, you gotta bring your passport to get through the casino doors. Despite these restrictions, Koreans are still known as gamblers and can become highly addicted to betting it all. No worries, though; what they can't get in their backyard is just a jet ride away in Las Vegas, which has become the all-time favorite tourist destination for Koreans.

Illegal gambling
Bulbeobdobak
불법도박

It's only illegal when you get caught gambling.
Dobageun hadaga japyeohsseulttae bulbeobiya.
도박은 하다가 잡혔을때 불법이야.

Bet
Geolgi
걸기

Do you want to bet money?
Don geollae?
돈 걸래?

Go stop
Go stop
고스톱

This game originated from Japan using cards called Hwatoo. Three players and a banker play. Whoever collects the most matching cards wins the game.

Ah, I have the shitty card!
A, tto ssanne!
아, 또 쌌네!

You're short with your point!
Pibage gwangbagine!
피박에 광박이네!

Jeongseon City
Jeongseon
정선

This town is like the Korean Las Vegas, but it's strictly regulated, and you're allowed to enter only three times a month. They check your ID and keep records on how much you spend. But it's not nearly as glamorous as its American counterpart, and the only free drink you'll get is soda. They're trying to make it a more fun destination by building new resorts, but if you're really itching to gamble, Seoul is still your best bet.

Horseracing
Gyeongma
경마
There is a limit on how much you can bet, normally up to 500,000 won ($500).

Bike racing
Gyeongryunjang
경륜장
Yes, there is bike racing that you can go watch and bet on.

Bullfighting
Sossaum
소싸움
This is not like Spanish or Mexican bullfighting—no Korean is dumb enough to jump into a ring with a bull. Korean bullfighting, usually held in the countryside, pits two bulls against each other.

CHAPTER 9

HUNGRY KOREAN

HANGUKESEO BAEGOPEULTTAE HANEUNMAL

한국에서 배고플때 하는말

If you're a vegetarian or vegan, don't come to Korea. Just don't. Korea is a meat country, and if you're not down with that, GTFO. Because of this carnivorous spirit, BBQ is big in Korea—and ridiculously delicious—but it can be pricey, mainly because Korean beef is almost three times more expensive than American beef. So you'll usually find pork being served as the meat of choice at these restaurants. The best Korean BBQ comes from the little hole-in-the-walls that you'll find in any city. Be sure to check one out for an authentic Korean experience.

Even bigger than BBQ is pork belly slices (*samgyeopsal*; 삼겹살). Koreans just loooooove this. And dog meat, though not eaten by a large percentage of people, and technically illegal, is still consumed by a small minority—which, though kind of disgusting, adequately shows you just how much Koreans really, really love their meat.

But of course, man cannot live on meat alone. And that's where rice comes in. Despite a steady decline in the country's rice consumption, Koreans still eat everything with rice. And by everything, I do mean everything. No matter what or when you're eating—be it breakfast, lunch or dinner—it's gonna come with rice.

·····Hunger
Baegopeum
배고픔

I'm starving.
Baegopa.
배고파.

I am dying of hunger.
Na baegopa jukkesseo.
나 배고파 죽겠어.

I am dying of thirst.
Na mok malla jukkesseo.
나 목 말라 죽겠어.

Let's eat!
Bab meokja!
밥 먹자!

I could go for some...
Na ... meokgosipeo.
나 ... 먹고싶어.

> **food.**
> *eumsik*
> 음식

> **chow.**
> *meogeulkkeo*
> 먹을거

drinks.
masilkkeo
마실거

beverages.
eumryosu
음료수

street food.
gilgeori eumsik
길거리 음식

junk food.
bullyang sikpum
불량식품

fast food.
fast food
페스트 푸드

a sumptuous feast. (also indicates a variety of dishes)
jinsuseongchan
진수성찬

a good meal.
masinneun eumsik
맛있는 음식

healthy food.
geongangsik
건강식

Korean BBQ.
cheolpangui / sutbulgyi
천판구이 / 숯불구이
Koreans love beef and pork, but because beef is expensive, the most common meat at a Korean BBQ is pork.

Chinese food.
Junguk eumsik
중국음식
You can also use *jjankkae* (짱개), which is slangier.

delivery service.
baedal
배달
Almost all restaurants in Korea will deliver takeout without any extra fee or tip. Most delivery boys use motorcycles fitted with stainless steel carriers called *cheolgabang* (철가방). These spacious cases with interior shelves for stacking plates are so synonymous with delivery service that the word has also become slang for the delivery guys.

all-you-can-eat buffet.
muhan refill
무한 리필
Some of these pig-out restaurants have a one-hour time limit. To get your money's worth of chow, you'd better learn to quickly stuff your face. It's not so hard to eat fast in Korea, since everyone likes to get things done quickly.

I'm full.
Baebulleo.
배불러.

I'm stuffed to my neck.
Mokkaji kkwak chasseo.
목까지 꽉 찼어.

I'm going to throw up.
To nawa.
토 나와.

I'm going to burst.
Bae teojigesseo.
배 터지겠어.

Thanks for the meal. (before the meal)
Jal meokkeseupnida.
잘 먹겠습니다.
It's considered polite to announce that you are thankful for the meal when someone buys you food.

Thanks for the meal. (after the meal)
Jal meogeosseupnida.
잘 먹었습니다.

•••••Delicious
Jinjja masisseo
진짜 맛있어

Really tasty.
Mat jota.
맛 좋다.

It melts in my mouth.
Hyeoe salsal nokneunda.
혀에 살살 녹는다.
This is useful when you have really good sashimi.

It was really good.
Neomu masisseosseo.
너무 맛있었어.

Yum yum.
Yamyam jjeopjjeop.
얌얌 쩝쩝.

It's sweet and spicy.
Maekomhada.
매콤하다.

It warms up my body. (hot soup)
Eolkeunhada.
얼큰하다.

PICKY EATERS)))
PYEONSIK
편식

It's very common for parents to nag their children into eating all their food, especially vegetables. These are some of the phrases you might hear as mothers attempt to coerce/guilt/scare their picky children into eating what's good for them. You may also use it on your anorexic Korean girlfriend to get extra meat on her!

You will be punished if you don't finish your meal.
Eumsik namgimyeon beolbada.
음식 낡기면 벌받아.

You won't grow if you don't eat this.
Neo igeo an meogeumyeon ki ankeunda.
너 이거 안 먹으면 키 안큰다.

Don't be picky and eat everything.
Neo pyeonsikhajimalgo golgoru meogeo.
너 편식하지않고 골고루 먹어.

Filling
Bae chewojinda
배 체워진다

I am going to order more.
Chugayo.
추가요.

·····Yuck!
Uek!
우엑!

Gross!
Deoreowo!
더러워!

This place sucks!
Yeogi mateopsseo!
여기 맛없어!

What a waste of money.
Doni neomu akkapda.
돈이 너무 아깝다.

It's disgusting.
Igeo yeokgyeowo.
이거 역겨워.

It's dirty in there.
Geu gage jijeobunhae.
그 가게 지저분해.

It's so-so.
Geu gage geunyang geurae.
그 가게 그냥 그래.

It's too pricey and not good enough.
Bissagiman hae.
비싸기만 해.

•••••At the restaurant
Eumsikjeomeseo
음식점에서

Restaurant service in Korea is generally top-notch. And as a wallet-friendly bonus, the food is really cheap. You can get a gourmet, home-cooked meal for the price of a latte. And the tax and tip are often included, as are constant refills of side dishes called *banchan* (반찬). Most small restaurants don't accept credit cards—cash is king. They also won't bring you a check unless you request it.

Another thing to remember: Don't sit around waiting for your server to take your order or clear your plate; you're expected to call them anytime you want them. Just don't be a dick about it, though—call them *eonni* (언니; "sister"), or *imo* (이모; "aunt"), in a friendly way. And don't try to tip servers in Korea, because they might find it insulting. On the other hand, you can't be too picky about your food. Korean restaurants aren't like Burger King: You don't get to have it your way. They don't like to substitute or leave out ingredients for you. And it's not common to ask for to-go or doggy bags, either.

Excuse me!
Jeogiyo!
저기요!

Over here!
Yeogiyo!
여기요!
This is more commonly used than "excuse me" to call the wait staff. Servers in Korea won't come to you unless you raise your hand and yell to get their attention!

Can we order?
Jumuniyo.
주문이요.
Literally, "Get my order."

What do you recommend?
Yeogi moga jeil masisseoyo?
여기 뭐가 제일 맛있어요?

How much is this?
Igeo eolmayaeyo?
이거 얼마예요?

How big is the portion?
Yangi eottaeyo?
양이 어때요?

What's in this?
Yeogi moga deureoisseoyo?
여기 뭐가 들어있어요?

Can I get this?
Igeo juseyo.
이거 주세요.

Can I get a menu?
Menupan juseyo.
매뉴판 주세요.

Can I get some water?
Mul jom juseyo.
물 좀 주세요.

Give me my bill.
Gyesanseo juseyo.
계산서 주세요.

Let's go Dutch.
Dutch pay haja.
더치 페이 하자.

Older Koreans traditionally take bills and pay for a whole table.
However, the younger generation has adopted the custom of
paying for oneself—mostly in an effort to save people from going
broke. If you're taking a girl out on a date, though, don't be a
cheap bastard. Guys are still expected to treat.

·····Popular Korean food
Hangukeui yumyeonghan yori
한국의 유명한 요리

I love Korean food, and it's not just because I'm Korean. OK,
maybe it is, but even non-natives will be amazed at the variety
of offerings. The following are some of the tastiest and most
popular dishes you'll encounter in your travels.

Rice
Bap
밥

White rice is the country's main staple and is served in most
Korean restaurants. Rice is so integral to the Korean diet, it's also
a synonym for "food."

Mixed-grain rice

Japgokbap

잡곡밥

If you visit your Korean friend's family, you'll likely be served a multi-grained mix of rice.

Kimchi

Kimchi

김치

This is the most famous Korean side dish. The most well-known to Westerners is the fiery pickled-cabbage variety, but in reality there are more than 50 kinds of kimchis. Don't be afraid to try other variations made with turnips, cucumbers and onions—not all of them are spicy.

Ramen

Ramyeon

라면

Most Korean ramen consists of instant noodles that come in various flavors. It's been said that one university student lived off ramen for a month and died from lack of nutrients. So, I don't recommend eating too many packages, but it's good and cheap food for curing a hangover!

Udon

Udong

우동

This Japanese noodle soup is really popular in Korea.

Fried fish cakes

Odaeng

오댕

These fried fish cakes, served on a stick, are some of the most popular street foods in Korea. You may also see a sliced version show up in the myriad side dishes brought to the table at a Korean BBQ.

Seaweed rice roll

Kimbap

김밥

Kimbap is a Korean sushi roll. Mothers pack them for children's field trips—or if you have a lazy mom, she'll give you the 1,000 won (about a $1) it costs to just buy one.

Tempura

Twigim

튀김

Fried food is universally yummy. Even skinny Koreans can't resist the allure of crispy, greasy treats.

Spicy rice cake

Ddeokbeokgi

떡복기

This rice cake dish, flavored with *gochujjang* (고추장)—a condiment made with red chilies and fermented soybeans—is perfect for big groups of people at street vendors.

Pig-intestine noodle (Korean sausage)

Sundae

순대

I know it sounds gross, but it's one of the tastiest foods I've ever tried. The sausage is stuffed with clear noodles then soaked in pig blood to get its authentic and unique flavor. The dish also comes with a side of pig's ears, intestines and liver. Oink, oink!

Bibimbap

비빔밥

Literally, "mixed rice." A combination of fresh vegetables and marinated meat with rice that you mix with *gochujjang*.

Black bean noodles

Jjajangmyeon

짜장면

This dish uses the same fermented and salted black beans as seen in Chinese cookery, but *jjajang* (짜장) served over noodles is much thicker than the Chinese version.

Jjambbong
짬뽕

A spicy noodle soup with seafood, *jjambbong* is a Chinese-Korean dish that's served in all Chinese restaurants in Korea.

Sushi
Chobap
초밥

Koreans typically like their sushi served nigiri style (raw fish over rice). However, ever since California rolls have become popular in Korea, there have been a lot more fusion maki rolls invented by Korean sushi chefs. How about maki sushi smothered in a sweet yogurt sauce? It just might be your next favorite thing to eat.

Sashimi
Hoe
회

Koreans use a spicy sauce called *chogouchujjang* (초고추장) for sashimi instead of the traditional wasabi.

Live sashimi
Hwareohoe
활어회

You choose a fish from a tank outside the restaurant; the live fish is then prepared for you on the spot. Expect a much thinner cut of sashimi than you're used to in the U.S.—the fresh flesh is so chewy, a thicker slice would make it harder to eat.

Pho
Weolnam guksu
윋남국수

Vietnamese rice noodle soup with sliced beef.

Beef stew
Seolleongtang
설렁탕

Oxtail soup, normally boiled for a day to get all the rich calcium from the bone.

Pizza

Pizza

피자

If you're sick and tired of eating Korean BBQ with rice and crave some American food like pizza, you might not quite get what you're looking for. Pizza in Korea is healthy compared to the U.S. counterpart—it's less greasy and has more nutritious toppings, such as king shrimp, squid and corn.

Pig's feet

Jokbal

족발

Boiled pig

Bossam

보쌈

Chinese cabbage wrap with tender broiled pork.

Dog stew

Bosintang

보신탕

The concept of dog stew sounds pretty repugnant to Americans—most Koreans, too. But those who do eat the canine concoction do so in the belief that it restores health, which is reflected in the dish's name: *Bosin* literally means "restoring health to the body."

Sliced rice pasta soup

Tteokguk

떡국

Traditional rice cake soup eaten on Lunar New Year's Day.

Dumpling soup

Manduguk

만두국

Soft tofu soup

Sundubu

순두부

Kimchi soup

Kimchijjigae

긴치찌개

This spicy savory dish is traditionally prepared with pork, but don't be surprised to see pink slices of SPAM floating in the broth when prepared by the home cook. Sounds kinda gross, but it's not. Who would have thought that kimchi and SPAM could go so well together?

Seaweed soup

Miyeokguk

미역국

Koreans always have this on their birthdays. Women who've just given birth also consume this tasty broth, which is high in calcium and iron. Presto—the association with birthdays.

Korean pancake

Buchimgae

부침개

A savory, wheat flour pancake served as an appetizer or snack. It can include kimchi (surprise), green onions or even squid. The plain ones with just green onions are called *pajeon* (파전); they are good with soy sauce.

Shaved ice

Patbingsu

팥빙수

Shaved ice with red bean sauce, topped with mochi balls and fruit. It's the bomb.

Fried chicken

Tongdak

통닭

I don't want to brag, but Koreans fry one mean motherfucking chicken!

·····Fast food
Fast food
패스트 푸드

Bunsikjeom
분식점
These Korean fast-food restaurants are like gourmet AM/PMs.
You can get food freshly cooked in front of you, or just pick up
some convenient and cheap Korean pre-packaged grub.

McDonald's
맥도날드

KFC
케이에프씨

Burger King
버거킹

Popeye's
파파이스

Lotteria
롯데리아
This Japanese franchise is the McDonald's of Korea.

Kimbapcheonguk
김밥천국
Popular chain serving quick, cheap Korean food.

Kyochon Chicken
교촌치킨
Popular franchise serving chicken with sweet and spicy
seasoning.

Two Two Chicken
둘둘치킨
I am not a big fried-chicken fan, but damn this is legit!

Mr. Pizza
미스터 피자

This is the most famous pizza chain in the country. Nice native twist: The crust here is made out of sweet potato.

Red Mango
레드 망고

Italy has their gelato. Americans have their ice cream. Koreans have their frozen yogurt. Red Mango is the most well-known of Korean yogurt chains and has even become successful in the U.S.

·····Cafés
Cafe
카페

Cafés in Korea are very fancy. American franchises like Starbucks are just like the ones in the U.S. However, you'll find some Korean twists at the native coffeehouse chains—latte flavors such as sweet potato and green tea cater to a decidedly Asian palate.

Should we go to a coffee shop to talk?
Uri coffee shope gaseo yaegihalkka?
우리 커피숖에 가서 얘기할까?

Let's go to a…
… gaja.
… 가자.

Korean country coffee shop.
Dabang
다방

There aren't many *dabangs* left these days, but in those that are still around, you'll often find your coffee accompanied by a lady of loose morals, if you catch my drift. Coffee and hookers: a winning combination!

Starbucks.
Stabucks
스타벅스
Koreans also call this *byeoldabang* (별다방), literally meaning "star coffee shop."

Coffee Bean.
Coffee Bean
커피빈
Also shortened to just *kongdabang* (콩다방), literally meaning "bean coffee shop."

Pendalion's Nostalgia.
Mindeulle Yeongto
민들레 영토
Located all around university campuses, these cafés provide private study rooms and unlimited coffee refills. Most students like to stick around and study for a few hours. They're cool, but a bit expensive.

·····Other Ulysses Press Titles

Dirty Chinese: Everyday Slang from "What's Up?" to "F*%# Off!"
MATT COLEMAN & EDMUND BACKHOUSE, **$10.00**

Dirty Chinese includes phrases for every situation, even expressions to convince a local official that you have waited long enough and tipped him plenty already. A pronunciation guide, a reference dictionary and sample dialogues make this guide invaluable for those traveling to China.

Dirty French: Everyday Slang from "What's Up?" to "F*%# Off!"
ADRIEN CLAUTRIER & HENRY ROWE, **$10.00**

With this book, you can use sweet words to entice a local beauty into a walk along the Seine, and less-than-philosophical rebuffs for those zealous, espresso-fueled cafe "poets." There are enough insults and swear words to offend every person in France without even speaking to them in English.

Dirty German: Everyday Slang from "What's Up?" to "F*%# Off!"
DANIEL CHAFFEY, **$10.00**

Dirty German provides plenty of insults and swear words to piss off every person in Germany—without even mentioning that the Japanese make better cars—as well as explicit sex terms that'll even embarrass the women of Hamburg's infamous red light district.

Dirty Italian: Everyday Slang from "What's Up?" to "F*%# Off!"
GABRIELLE EUVINO, **$10.00**

This useful guide contains phrases for every situation, including insults to hurl at the refs during *fútbol* games. Readers learn sweet words to entice a local beauty into a romantic gondola ride, not-so-sweet remarks to ward off any overzealous Venetians, and more.

Dirty Japanese: Everyday Slang from "What's Up?" to "F*%# Off!"
MATT FARGO, **$10.00**

Even in traditionally minded Japan, slang from its edgy pop culture constantly enter into common usage. This book fills in the gap between how people really talk in Japan and what Japanese language students are taught.

Dirty Russian: Everyday Slang from "What's Up?" to "F*%# Off!"
ERIN COYNE & IGOR FISUN, **$10.00**

An invaluable guide for off-the-beaten-path travelers going to Russia, *Dirty Russian* is packed with enough insults and swear words to offend every person in Russia without even mentioning that they lost the Cold War.

Dirty Spanish: Everyday Slang from "What's Up?" to "F*%# Off!"
JUAN CABALLERO & NICK DENTON-BROWN, **$10.00**

This handbook features slang for both Spain and Latin America. It includes a section on native banter that will help readers make friends over a pitcher of sangría and convince the local taco maker that it's OK to spice things up with a few fresh habaneros.

To order these books call 800-377-2542 or 510-601-8301, fax 510-601-8307, e-mail ulysses@ulyssespress.com, or write to Ulysses Press, P.O. Box 3440, Berkeley, CA 94703. All retail orders are shipped free of charge. California residents must include sales tax. Allow two to three weeks for delivery.